Park Street Angels

Park Street Angels

A Chronicle of Hope

CHRISTINA NORDSTROM

ISBN: Softcover   978-1-5434-2232-0
              eBook   978-1-5434-2231-3

Print information available on the last page.

Revision date: 05/16/2017

To order additional copies of this book, contact:
Xlibris
1-888-795-4274
www.Xlibris.com
Orders@Xlibris.com
761751

CONTENTS

"Do not neglect to show hospitality to strangers, for, by doing that, some have entertained angels without knowing it."

Part I

Introduction

After a very successful career in health education spanning some 20-odd years, in the spring of 2003 at the age of 52, I ended up as what I refer to as collateral damage in the raging war of healthcare economics. I was [then] directing a health education outreach program for a community hospital and had just completed a graduate program in instructional design. Early in the new millennium, funding for "prevention" activities succumbed to economic pressures and had to take a back seat to essential [and reimbursable] direct patient care. From a purely pragmatic standpoint, reality dictated that, while health education and prevention programs were necessary, they also needed to be provided in a more cost-effective manner – through outsourcing. So my position was discontinued.

A friend referred to this time in my life as "patchwork time." I had pieced together several part-time employment situations, including serving as executive director for a small human service agency and picking up private consulting work writing grant proposals, to fill 40 or so working hours a week. However, my "ends" never quite met – they always seemed to fray, sometimes right along with my nerves. While seeking full-time employment I kept bumping up against what my sister refers to as the "glass window" – an invisible barrier that prevents middle-agers like us from finding employment. It adds yet another challenge to the crisis [or "opportunity," depending on "the lenses through which you view the world"] of mid-life.

As some of my part-time activities concluded, by the fall of 2005 I was working only 10 hours a week. Having lived paycheck to paycheck all my life, I didn't have one of those financial cushions for life's rainy days. But, it was starting to rain, and I was getting wet.

I took an inventory and considered my options, particularly for another, more affordable living arrangement. Those who know me know that I cherish my living space, and that to decide to move would be an act of desperation. I tried to reduce expenses and take advantage of services for which I was now eligible. The years during which I worked within the "human service" industry served me well in that I knew where to look for fuel assistance and other support services in my town. My situation also allowed me to receive partial unemployment compensation.

Applying for unemployment was relatively easy. I could be somewhat anonymous over the phone – I didn't actually have to face anyone. I just had to provide information to verify past employment and so forth. But when it came to applying for fuel and utility assistance, it was a much more sobering [and, frankly, embarrassing] task. I had to do this in person. When I finally worked up my courage to go to the local agency that took care of people like me, which was housed at my town's Council on Aging facility, it was hard to be anonymous. But, by the grace of God, a friend from my church was volunteering there that day. Many of us refer to her as an "angel"; she always knows what to do or say. Sometime it's just enough that she's there. So, while I wasn't anonymous, I felt supported; I wasn't alone.

Sitting figuratively and literally on "the other side of the desk," I talked about my situation with the case manager and was given "reams" of forms to document my expenses and how much, or – adding insult to injury – how little I was making. While I had done it before in my imagination (in "experience-walking-in-the-other-guy's-shoes" assignments in human service classes, and in my song writing), it was humbling to think about actually putting on "the shoes." *Mortifying* and *humiliating* might be better words. Continuing the metaphor, I now found myself *shopping in the same store.*

Having graduated from the College of Public and Community Service at UMASS Boston with a degree in Human Services Management, I have supported "many things just" in my adult life. Also, growing up in the 60's, I'd learned how to be an advocate – on someone else's behalf or for some important cause. But, when it comes to standing up and advocating for my own needs, that's a whole other thing. It's just plain hard, embarrassing and demeaning to ask. I felt ashamed. Maybe it's because I was still in so much denial that this was happening in the first place. Maybe it's because I felt like such a failure. "If only ..."

The case manager asked me to prove that I was eligible to apply for assistance. She showed me the financial eligibility chart. It was like receiving a reality-awakening punch in the gut when I saw the numbers. I was, unfortunately, *indeed* eligible. *"Across the table, in my humility,"* I wrote in a song about this episode in my life, *"there begged my ego that I may worthy be. What are the measures of poverty? Well, there, **with** the grace of God, am I."*

So, applying for unemployment compensation was OK, but applying for this other assistance was not. I was too ashamed to get the verification information that was required in order to process my application. It involved the agency having to check with other people, e.g., my landlord, about how much I paid for rent and utilities. He was already giving me a huge break in my rent, and I didn't want to go through the embarrassment of what, to me, was like asking him for more. So I rationalized that there must be someone else who needed the assistance more than I did. I didn't pursue it further. I let it drop.

But, while "ends" still weren't meeting, God's awesome grace worked through several friends and family members who helped me financially with loans and outright gifts – some given without my having to ask. It was just enough to help me get through the patchwork time. And, for me, there's a happy ending. In the spring of 2006 I found full-time employment in Boston directing the overweight prevention [or healthy weight promotion] program for the state. I finally broke through the "glass window." However, I won't forget the patchwork time in my life or about all the people who are still piecing their lives together.

Chapter 1

During the first weeks commuting to my new job in town, after emerging from the Park Street subway station in the heart of Boston, I would cross Tremont Street and walk down Winter to Downtown Crossing; then I'd take a left on Washington Street and walk a few more blocks. I didn't really know the area very well and hadn't ventured out much during my lunch [half-] hour to explore. Downtown Crossing at 7:30 a.m. is a messy brick-paved slalom course of over-stuffed blue plastic trash bins. But, after meeting my sister for supper in town after work one evening at the Parker House Hotel on the corner of Tremont and School Streets (which connected with Washington), I found a new route. The walk up School Street, passing by the site of the first public school and King's Chapel on the right, and left down Tremont Street, past the old Granary Burial ground, wherein *Mother Goose* and Paul Revere lie, and the Park Street Church along Boston's historical *Freedom Trail,* was a lot more pleasant. I used this more inspiring trail to and from work each day.

One day en [new] route to work, I noticed a man sitting in front of the Park Street Church. I passed him there every day for a few days, noticing him out of the corner of my eye to avoid becoming "engaged." He had white-grey hair, a beard and glasses which made him look kind of like a Dickensian St. Nicholas. But he was dressed in a T-shirt, jeans and a baseball cap like any contemporary of mine [OK, an old "hippie"]. From a short distance, I could read one of the hand-written signs that sat next to him on the sidewalk. It demanded: "SMILE: It's the Law." I obeyed the law, but kept walking.

After a few days of this, he caught me peeking and our eyes connected. I was afraid – I don't know why, because he was smiling – but, it's probably because I got caught. I glanced away quickly and kept on walking. Then I looked back over my shoulder and saw him still watching me through the wrought iron railing of the church steps. Ice blue and smiling, his eyes connected with mine again. But I kept walking. There was something about his eyes that stayed with me all that day. Then I wondered if they were trying to tell me something, and then I felt somewhat foolish. I imagined he might be some kind of angel – the kind that only some people could see, or one who is dressed like "any man" who crosses your path and has some kind of message or challenge for you. Anyway, I didn't stop as I didn't have any change handy, and I didn't want to take the time to take off my backpack, which had now become part of my daily wardrobe, to search for my purse and rummage around for spare change. I kept walking; tomorrow I would be better prepared.

Next morning at 7 a.m., as I sat on the black vinyl-upholstered bench on the train, I fished around in my purse inside my backpack and found a few quarters. I put my premeditated donation in my pocket and hoped that I would make good my intention; I hoped that I wouldn't get cold feet and walk on by if I saw the fellow at Park Street again. It's not as if you could just walk by and flip a few coins into a paper cup and keep walking; he was situated so that you had to *intentionally* walk over a few yards out of your way to get to him.

He didn't jingle coins aggressively in a paper cup like other folks on the street did. He had an old cigar box that sat in front of him on the sidewalk; a cane leaned on the church wall behind him. He never asked outright, "Can you spare any change?" He always just smiled and waved at folks, especially the children on their way to day care a few buildings away.

I made good my intention. After crossing Park Street, I walked over to him and handed him the quarters. He took them while gently, briefly holding on to the tips of my fingers; then he let them go. Maybe it was a way of requiring a connection. With a warm smile he said, "Thank you, Ma'am." I was a little nervous and muttered something like, "You're welcome ... take care." But what kind of *care* could be purchased for 75 cents? I was rather embarrassed. And during that transaction, I saw another sign next to him that said, "Homeless by Fire." That, too, stayed with me the whole day.

Well, this was the beginning of an unintended, unconventional friendship. I would look forward to emerging from the subway each day on my way to work and speak with him about the events that shaped his life. I found myself investing in him as "a neighbor."

As I thought about this fellow, I remembered an assignment in a class that I had taken some years ago, entitled, "Race and Class in Human Services" at the College of Public and Community Service at UMASS Boston. We had to assume the identity of someone who was completely unlike ourselves and keep a diary for two weeks living [in our imagination] as that person. I chose to be a homeless woman living on the streets of Boston in November – dreary, damp, bone-chilling-cold November in Boston. In my/her diary, I/she was half-dazed with cold, trying to figure out how to take care of my/her personal needs, let alone find food to eat or some place for shelter. It did, indeed, make me think about things differently – an important lesson, not only for folks working in human services, but for *any*one living in "Life 101."

Walking in Boston each day, I encounter so many of these seemingly invisible souls. But, they're everywhere – people like this fellow who are disabled and out of work or just down on their luck. Others are suffering from addictions and still others are mentally or emotionally disabled, but left to fend for themselves on the streets and in shelters. They're not only on the streets, but they're overpopulating the state's correctional facilities as I learned in the world of AIDS and corrections. These most vulnerable souls remain unseen. We all walk by and don't see them sleeping on the steps of the church or on the sidewalk below. No matter what the season, there are souls lying there on or under thick grey wool blankets, the kind that we purchase for needy folks on "Blanket Sunday" in our church in suburban Boston in honor or in memory of our mothers on Mother's Day. These fragile blanketed souls are strewn across Boston Common near the Park Street "T" each morning.

I am, at the same time, grateful but not just a little frustrated and angry that I am beginning to see them. I'm angry because we as a society haven't figured out how to care "for the least of these." I remember one older, disabled woman who was parked at the top of the stairs of the Park Street "T" exit in her wheelchair. Her legs were covered with a blanket. She didn't have a paper cup and wasn't asking for money. She just sat there with her eyes cast downward and a vacant look on her face. When I finished climbing the stairs, I saw her and thought to myself that she must be one of the Park Street Angels. She didn't look up at me, but, then she smiled as I passed by as if to acknowledge that I had learned, and that she would trust me with her secret.

I wondered if this was her "work." Just to *be*, to be *there* in the midst of life's routines and daily chaos to make people like me consider the question, "Who is my neighbor?" Then I thought how cruel that would be and how dare I "romanticize" such a life. I recalled my pastor's words, paraphrased from Reverend James Forbes, from a recent sermon that challenged: "In order to get into heaven, you need a note from the poor."

How can I be her neighbor?

Chapter 2

I wished that I were a better conversationalist. I've never been good at starting conversations. I'm intolerant of small talk; it's too superficial and a waste of words. I prefer to discuss things that really matter. But getting to what really matters is not easy; it takes time establishing a relationship, and most times I'm too guarded anyway.

As the days went on, I wondered about how to begin a conversation with this curious fellow. I kept thinking about it and stayed open to any suggestions that might come to mind. I kept "listening" and came up with the words, "I'm sorry for your trouble." Next day, I would be prepared with words. And I found a couple of dollars to "spare."

When I saw him, I handed him the money and said, "I'm sorry for your trouble." He appreciated my acknowledgment and said, "Thank you." I walked on. Next day more words for questions came. I asked him about what he did for a living before the fire and all. He told me he worked as a roofer, with copper and slate on church roofs and steeples, when he was younger with his father and "his people." He'd eat "a man's breakfast" of eggs and bacon each day. He said that now he was the only one in his family left; everyone else was gone. He lost everything in the fire, including tools and templates that he and his dad would use for making and selling copper lanterns. I asked him what he'd rather be doing than sitting on a plastic milk crate each day outside the church. He said, "I'd *work*." But with badly controlled diabetes, which created other health problems, he was on disability. He said, "This is all that I can do now."

Not wanting to pry, but because I'm becoming more interested in knowing about his life, I asked him, "Where did you stay at night when you first became homeless?"

He didn't mind that I asked, saying that, "Many times I'd stay in the subway. It was safer than in being in the shelters as most of the guys there would be drunk or they'd be doing drugs or they'd steal from each other." He said, "I'd rather take my chances in the subway."

"Do the 'T' police give you any trouble?" I asked

"Oh, no, not me," he answered. "It's all about my attitude. I don't drink and become belligerent like the others, so they leave me alone."

Thinking I might be helpful, I asked, "Where do you get your care for the diabetes?"

He answered, "I know some friendly doctors over at MGH." He told me that they took care of him especially one time when he had a serious problem with it. He remarked that while he was a patient there, they had a tough time controlling his sugar levels and gave him insulin four times a day. He also noted that when he ate the right foods, to which he had access while he was in the hospital, it had the [remarkable] result of helping keep it under better control. But, for him, *that he had access to food at all* after he left the hospital was a continuing problem. He said it was hard to test his blood and many of his meals consisted of others' discarded table scraps that he fished out of garbage cans. He said he once grew potatoes near where he and some other folks sheltered under one of the bridges in town.

I wondered about faith and what does this kind of life circumstance do to a person's faith. But I didn't ask him about it. What strange juxtaposition, I thought, for me to be working with an obesity prevention program to help people *stop eating so much* while every day encountering a human being who subsists on garbage and who knows that he can control his diabetes by eating good food. If he had access to good food, perhaps then he wouldn't have to depend on the health care system to pay for so much treatment. Irony – sheer irony.

Chapter 3

On Friday, "SMILE: It's the Law" changed to "SMILE: It's *Friday*." As I approached, and before I could say good morning to him, he said: "One rattle snake was talking to another one and asked, 'Are we poisonous?' The other rattler said, 'Yes, we are.' The first snake said, 'Uh, oh!' and the second, 'What's the matter?' to which the first one replied, 'I just bit my tongue!'" A smile spread across my face and I didn't feel nervous around him any longer.

Another day as I approached, before we could exchange greetings, he pointed to a red-tailed hawk perched atop a tall building across the street. He had also placed a large white clamshell filled with birdseed for the sparrows in front of him on the sidewalk. "They have to eat, too." He was frustrated as he alternately shooed away a pigeon and then a squirrel who were both trying to steal some seed. He grumbled that doing so took away from the time he had to spend "doing whatever it is I'm supposed to be doing here."

Each day I would try to ask more questions. In one of my lunchtime walks, I came across a veterans' shelter, just a few blocks away from the Park Street Church near Government Center. Was he a veteran I asked? Yes, he was, but he would have no part of the services they offered. The [Vietnam] war was responsible for killing his brother, Richard. He was still angry and I sensed he was still grieving. He told me about how as children he and Richard were "routinely" escorted by a social worker – each with one hand holding on to a small black suitcase and the other holding on to one of the social worker's hands – from foster home to foster home. He said they never knew why they had to leave each time, but it taught him not to trust or depend on anyone. He said he never was able to get close to a family because it never lasted anyway. His mother was not in his life as a child and I'm still not clear about his father's role in his life – only that they ended up working together.

Once, after several weeks of meeting there in the morning, he said, partly kidding but partly serious, "I'm afraid of people like you. You're here one day and then gone the next." I told him that this is the way I go to work each day – one day at a time. I told him that in a difficult and needy time in my life, some friends and family members had helped me out – some without my asking because they knew how hard it was to ask. Some had been "there" before themselves. I said I wanted to do the same, as I knew only half an *inkling* about living through hardship. (To help out, a friend and I had taken up the routine of providing him with supermarket gift cards each week.) I knew also that sometimes their kindness in just being with me and letting me talk things out was all I needed to keep moving forward, inch by little inch.

I remembered a time when I was newly separated, working full-time and taking care of my toddler son. While we had a roof over our heads, I remember a wintry Saturday when it was time to go food shopping. Because "ends" didn't meet then either, I broke open my son's piggy bank and counted out twelve dollars in pennies, dimes and nickels to buy some food until next payday. I didn't know how to ask for what I needed then. I'm still learning.

Our almost-daily meetings continued. Even if it was raining and I could take a stop closer to work, I would go to the Park Street stop. For me it was more important to be consistent, to show up one day at a time.

Chapter 4

Mr. Margolis often sports a different hat every time I see him. He had known my Park Street Church friend for some time now. My new friend was always very formal with names – Mr. This or Mrs. That. I would later learn that we both came from the same era; that's what we were taught. We were also, as I recall, taught to "be seen and not heard." Anyway, while it was hard for him to do so, he would also usually stand up, leaning against the church wall for balance, out of respect when Mr. Margolis approached. Sometimes he would do that for me, too, but he said his feet often hurt too much. I always told him not to get up when he made the attempt.

"Hi, Bob," said Mr. Margolis as he greeted him. I never thought to ask Bob's name, and I never introduced myself to him either for that matter. But I was glad now to know it and to also let him know mine. Bob said, "This is Mr. Margolis," and I introduced myself as Chris. So now we all knew each other's names.

Mr. Margolis had known and had been helping Bob for a couple of years, sometimes with significant essentials. Sometimes he coached Bob on how to approach "the system" to advocate for himself. He shared some cash and clever conversation with Bob each time he'd stop by. I really like clever words, and enjoyed being part of their conversations. Bob told me that Mr. Margolis was a lawyer and he worked down the street in Government Center.

Chapter 5

One memorable morning I approached him with my usual greeting. He said, "Hello, Sunshine." (I'm glad I can brighten *some*one's day!) He fished around in his backpack and produced and presented a "coupon" that he had hand-designed. On all four corners was written: *"Free Pass."* Then he had written the following:

> *Notice to Bearer: Should I, Homeless Bob, arrive at Heaven's gate before you, you may cut in front of me. Notice to St. Pete (A.K.A. Gate Keeper): The bearer of this pass has excelled in treating the homeless with respect. Signed, Homeless Bob, Homeless by Fire.*

I got my "note"!

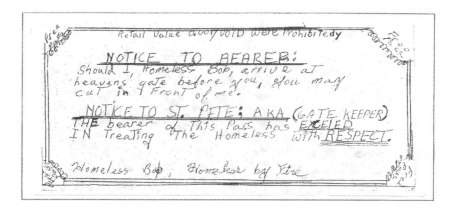

Chapter 6

If you're clever [and I like to think that I am], commuting on the "T" can be productive, particularly for an aspiring songwriter.

For example, I don't particularly like the look of toes – mine or anyone else's. But, summertime brings them out in full force, cradled in myriad varieties of flimsy, flip-floppy, fantasy and [questionably] fashionable footwear. It's not only my fellow commuters' foot gear that's so fanciful, sometimes it's the toes themselves! While riding the subway to work each day, I usually sit and stay in my own thoughts. My eyes are cast downward (sometimes I snooze) for the 30-minute ride that links the suburbs to the city. What a spectacle there is to be seen!

Toes

There are dainty, painted, peeking-through-silky-salmon-satin-toe-hole toes;
Tiny, candy-red-tipped, poking-through-frilly-flowered-flip-flops toes;
Oyster-shell-lacquered, suffering-'neath-the-weight-of-
ice-blue-crystal-mock-rock-studded-sandals toes;
Rouge, blanc et bleu French-tipped-to-match-their-red-white-and-blue-sandals toes.

And there are prestidigitated digits concealed in fatigued army-camouflaged sandals;
Elongated, red-punctuated, brown-bronzed, thong-entwined toes;
Once-new-and-nimble-now-numb-and-neuropathetic toes;
Much-too-swollen-and-stuffed-into-my-conservative-shoes-for-comfort toes [mine].

Then there are can't-you-tell-I-haven't-washed-my-feet-in-several-days toes;
Soft, pink, unadulterated, innocent and naked toes;
Bound, bent, bunionated, bruised and blistered toes;
Wiggling-out-of-my-pointy-spike-heels-to-oh-so-comfortable-flip-flops toes!
Maybe I should look up more. I really love the fall.

Then I thought that maybe I should, indeed, look up more. Next day on the "T," I was determined to do so. I saw a man sitting directly across from me, very straight and tall, in dark glasses wearing a navy blue baseball cap with an air force emblem. I couldn't tell if he was sleeping, staring at me or out the window. He was motionless for most of the trip except for when his gaze [or snooze] was interrupted by incoming herds of morning commuters along the way.

Looking up higher, I saw advertisements with poorly written slogans. I wondered at the opportunity that was missed to help people learn to proper*ly* speak the English language [or should that be "speak the English language properly"?]. Not that I'm any expert, but it's just a pet peeve of mine. And isn't it just as easy to print "GO SLOWLY" on a street sign as it is to print "GO SLOW"? Gee, what if they added the word, "PLEASE"? And couldn't we come up with something better – don't we *deserve* something better – than the challenging, *in-your-face* electronic highway message: "YOU DRINK, YOU DRIVE, YOU LOSE"?

Anyway, continuing with the exercise, as I looked up I saw people standing reading their papers or fiddling with *IPOD*s. Some were defying the laws of gravity and physics by not holding on to *any*thing and expecting to stay upright when the train lurched to a sudden stop. Heads bobbed in their morning books, newspapers or snoozes and exposed everything from crooked-parted coiffures [why can't people part their hair in a straight line anymore!?] to shiny, balding, bronzed brows. One "do" on one young woman's head seemed to be permanently subjected to a stiff breeze – like the ones that I've heard about in Aruba. It was combed over and "glued" so that it stuck out sideways, sweeping from left to right I thought it was important that she sat on the train with her head going in the right direction or one might get somewhat disoriented when looking at her.

In another season, if I were to look across the subway car and out the window, the trees and buildings outside would be flying by at about 60 miles per hour. But, now in the summer, when the tracks overheat in the 100-degree-plus air, the world must go by a little more slowly.

At the JFK/UMASS stop, a very tall and muscular African American young man, with a serious look on his face and wearing a T-shirt and jeans, boarded the train. He sat next to me in the only seat left. He appeared to be in his early 20's, but I don't do well guessing ages. He was holding a tissue over a cut on his hand, and, as he kept peeking, it kept oozing. Should I offer help? I must have a Band-aid somewhere in my bag. But, I wonder what people will think?

Nobody else is doing anything. At South Station, the train was almost emptied of its "cargo." Still nursing his wound, the young man slid over so that there was a seat open between us, but it was soon filled with a new passenger. I was determined to find a Band-aid and scrounged around in my wallet as the train moved on. I knew I had one! But, it's one of the square patches and I wondered if it would be of any help. I hesitated. But then, without saying a word, I somewhat meekly leaned forward around the passenger sitting between us and offered him the bandage. The biggest smile beamed through his formerly somber countenance. He said, "Thank you. Thank you very much," and then applied it to the wound. His stop was next, and as he got up to leave, he stepped over in front of me and smiled again. "Thank you very much."

In August I started journaling about my meetings with Bob. I wanted to remember.

An undated entry in August, 2006

Emerging from the Park Street "T" it had become my habit to immediately look to see if Bob was sitting in his spot. When he's not feeling well, he usually doesn't make the subway trip from Revere. So I'm always glad when he's there, because it generally means he's OK. He was there today and greeted me with, "Good morning, Sunshine!" It's always nice to hear that. But, even though he was there, his mood was somewhat "down." He shared that sometimes it's just too hard and it takes so much time just to get clean [himself and his clothes] and then to find food to eat.

In spite of his "blues," he had a gift for me – it was a small digital camera in a case that someone had given him. He offered it to me with an operating manual that had been downloaded from the Internet. He said he didn't know how to figure it out and that it would probably get stolen anyway. I accepted it reluctantly and said that I'd just hold on to it for him, and if he wanted to use it, I'd get it back to him. I'd also have to get someone to help me figure it out. We chatted some more and then I had to get to work. I gave him the supermarket gift cards along with a "two-dollar handshake." I thanked him for the camera and wished him well. "See you tomorrow," he said. "Stay cool," I replied.

August 22, 2006

"Hi, Chris. You remember Mr. Margolis," Bob said as I approached this morning. Mr. Margolis had arrived before me. I had, indeed, remembered him. He was the one with the hats. In one of our conversations on a previous day, Mr. Margolis was wondering (in a mocking, upper-crusty accent) what sort of chapeau he should wear for an upcoming yachting event in Marblehead that he was expected [but it was apparent that he did not want] to attend. The song, *You're So Vain* came to mind. We all laughed.

I asked Bob how he had been feeling; he had been sick for several days and hadn't been out in his usual spot. He said he was feeling better and wondered if I had figured out how to use a camera. I told him that I hadn't yet because I, too, was rather technologically challenged. But I had a friend who I was asking to help me with it. I don't do well reading directions; I'm the kind of learner who needs someone to show me rather than tell me. Mr. Margolis agreed that it was much easier to learn that way.

August 29, 2006

Mr. Margolis was again finishing a conversation with Bob when I emerged from the Park Street underground. He was sporting a very heavily bandaged right forearm. I asked him what had happened, and he said, "I was attacked by a wild animal." Bob said it was his wife. Mr. Margolis said it was his cat. I wasn't sure which one of them to believe. Mr. Margolis said that it was wrapped that way more to protect it from further injury, and it looked worse than it really was. He tipped his hat and walked on to work, which, as Bob explained to me, was as a "civil rights lawyer." Bob said he had offered to take him for his annual eye examination soon which MassHealth would cover. Bob said that they treat him more respectfully when Mr. Margolis is with him.

Bob asked for information about foods to eat for someone who has diabetes. I suggested that he talk to his doctor when he saw her next, but I told him that I would pick up some information for him at work. He wasn't going to use his supermarket gift coupons until he knew the right foods to buy. I told him I would bring them by tomorrow when I saw him.

He had told me previously that, "if you want to help homeless folks, but if you didn't want to give them money, you could always give them a *Stop & Shop* gift card – those are the best – or make a sandwich or pack up leftovers from dinner and give them out the next day. In the winter they always need warm socks and underwear." He said he had been invited to speak at Suffolk University to talk to students there about his life and others who subsist in the streets. He's quite an advocate for the homeless.

Just then a young man with a white cane walked down Park Street, greeted Bob and went to the corner to wait for the light to cross to the "T" station. He was one of Bob's acquaintances. All of a sudden, Bob got up, looked at me and said, "Wait here." Feeling somewhat nervous about doing so, "wait [there]" I did. He limped over to the man, took his arm and waited with him for the white pedestrian signal. He walked him across the street to the entrance of the station. Then he limped back to his spot.

It was time for me to get to work. He wished me a good day with his signature smile.

August 31, 2006

Today's Bob's birthday. Robert George [I think is his middle name that I tried to remember from his ID card that he showed me to prove it] Wright was born in Portsmouth, New Hampshire on August 31, 1949. He's a little over a year older than I am, but you'd never know it. The stress of living really takes a toll. I met him this morning, but not in the usual place. I woke up at 3:30 a.m. and couldn't get back to sleep. So I got up and went through my routine that usually started at 4:30 a.m. and left the house an hour earlier. When I got to Park Street Church, he wasn't there – a guy with a video camera perched atop a tripod was in his place. [I supposed it was the guy he had told me about who was producing a video documentary of his life.] I walked down Tremont Street and all of a sudden I saw Bob walking toward me. He was using his cane and carried a backpack and milk crate; he was walking from the subway, from the Blue Line at Government center, I imagine, to the corner at the church. After a warm greeting, he asked why I was here so early. I told him I couldn't sleep and I had a lot of work to do. He said he was late today as he was finally *able* to sleep last night. It was a very cool late-August morning, and he was dressed in a very warm, hand-knit sweater that an acquaintance – I think he said she was a reference librarian – had given him. She also used to bring him leftovers.

He was concerned about me taking work home at night – I told him I didn't make it a regular practice. He wished me a good day. I told him that a man with a video camera was on "his" corner. He said that it must be Mr. Davis. So we said good-bye, I wished him another happy birthday, and we both went to "work."

Later that day...

There are so many themes that I am thinking about now, like in the *Book of Matthew*, "I was hungry and you gave me food, thirsty and you gave me something to drink ..." I feel angry and frustrated about Bob's circumstances and those of others like him. I have more questions than answers about all of this.

What would it take for our society to really help stop homelessness? Why can't we "get it" that it's really all about being brought up by nurturing parents and other care givers, as well as a supportive community, equitable access to healthcare and education, and having meaningful work opportunities so that children/youth/people develop a positive sense of self and *have a chance at* making positive contributions to their world – even if it does take some accommodation. [At a recent meeting at work, a colleague announced that there was a new study that confirmed that the cause of homelessness was poverty. A very large, but silent "*Duh?!*" hung over the conference table. I wonder how many thousands of dollars supported the research.]

Why do we throw billions toward rebuilding communities devastated by natural disasters – acute homelessness – while we haven't found a better way to meet the needs of the chronically homeless? Who are they anyway? What are the stories they would tell? Have they given up all hope? Are they too overwhelmed to hope?

In this country, why *can't* we provide folks with the "tools to fish" to become independent rather than keeping them dependent on receiving just "the fish dinner"?

Some say a country's success is measured by the way that it cares for its poor – for "the least of these..." So, who really is my neighbor? What should my investment be? Why do we romanticize the condition of the poor? Why is this country so greedy anyway?

September 1, 2006

Labor Day is coming up and I am looking forward to the long weekend ahead. Bob was in a "good place" today, and was very cheery. With a twinkle in his eye he admitted to looking forward to doing some girl watching on his corner on this warm, late-summer day. He told me not to miss the sand castle exhibit over the weekend on Revere Beach. "It's right at the end of the Blue Line," he said. He spent a lot of time at that beach during the summer. I thanked him for the tip but, good intentions notwithstanding, I decided to stay close to home and rest from my labors that had lately become all-consuming. But I saw coverage of the sand castles on a TV newscast over the weekend and thought of Bob being there and enjoying them.

The thought of the sand castles on Revere Beach reminded me of some we used to build as children further on up the coast at Goose Rocks Beach in Kennebunkport, Maine. They had inspired a song some years ago, which has a timeless theme:

Sand Castles

There are children building a castle on the Earth's ancient shore,
building a fortress to last through the centuries of war.
But, for all their skill and labor, despite their best-made plans,
the tide comes in and the fortress returns to tiny grains of sand.

There are children looking for heroes in this world to restore
a presence of hope for the fearful, for those who have borne
the despair and indifference caused by some cruel "slight of hand."
For some the choice is a light in the road, for some an empty hand.

Give the children hope for tomorrow through the gift of today.
Turn their anger and sorrow into laughter and play.
Teach them how to climb the mountain and live upon the land,
to build their house on solid ground and not upon the sand.

Give the children hope for tomorrow: give them today.
Turn your anger and sorrow into laughter and play
so that you can climb the mountain and live upon the land.
So build your house on solid ground – not upon the sand.

I think God intended for us to be heroes for our children.

An undated entry in September, 2006

Bob wasn't feeling very well when I stopped by today. Said it was due to diabetes, and he doesn't use the full dose of insulin that he's prescribed so he can make it last. I encouraged him to see his doctor, and he told me he'd try to get to see her in the "homeless clinic" at Massachusetts General Hospital; but she's only available there from 9 to 11 a.m. on Monday mornings. He related that he'd had two heart attacks before; at least two times on his corner he had been "carted away by ambulance" to the hospital. I told him that my friend, Sue, and I were concerned about him, that we wished we could do more. But he said that "you *are* doing something. You stop and talk to me instead of just walking by and ignoring me."

I recalled visiting with a group in El Salvador on one of several work-study trips to that country. I remember commenting to the *campesinos* in a parents group meeting that some of us felt frustrated that we couldn't offer anything substantial that might make a dent in making their living conditions more bearable. We were humbled when one of the fathers replied that we brought them hope. He said, "When you come to visit, you bring us hope. We feel as though we are not forgotten." I remember my aging mother who worries about being forgotten, too.

A fellow Bob knew walked by and they exchanged nods and smiles. Bob looked back at me, I pointed to his sign ("SMILE: It's the Law!"), and he smiled again. He said, "You know this is all just a façade." I knew. I presented the food gift cards, saying that Sue and I hoped they would help. He assured me they would, noting that he had had just a potato last night for supper.

Before Sue and I started giving him the gift cards, we had given him a gift card to *Bruggers Bagel Bakery*. I had remembered her kindness in giving me a card to Dunkin' Donuts. I remembered what it felt like *receiving* the gift during my *patchwork time* when buying coffee in a coffee shop was somewhat of an extravagance. I wanted to do the same for someone else. I told him the shop was nearby on School Street, just a couple of blocks away and he'd find it by following the *Freedom Trail*. A week or so later after he had gone there he commented about the cost of one meal – over eight dollars. He said he could get away eating for three dollars a day, not that he ate a lot for that amount.

But he was very frugal. So we liked giving him the cards to the supermarket, as it gave him more options. It gave him a *choice*.

I also gave him a birthday card with some birthday money that we had been waiting to give him since learning it was his birthday that week. He said, jokingly, that what he needed was a birthday "carr-r-r" (emphasizing the sound of "r") not a "card." I smiled and he did, too, as he said, "Thank you."

There are so many "invisible" angels strewn across Boston Common on these hot summer mornings. They're also "hidden" on the steps and in the nooks and crannies around Park Street Church. They must be invisible because no one "sees."

Who is my neighbor?

An undated entry in September, 2006

"Good morning, Sunshine!" was Bob's greeting today. His eyes had some of their sparkle back as he was feeling better. He was wearing his thick, warm sweater, which made me happy, and he had a blanket around his legs as he sat on the black plastic milk crate that doubled as a chair. I had interrupted his conversation with another gentleman, who lingered a bit while we were talking. Bob said that his blood pressure was "sky high" (he had been given a meter to use to keep track of it) and said he could feel his heart pounding. I asked him if he was going to get someone to look at him *today*. He said that he would. I asked him if I could get him anything, pointing to the *7-11* store across the street. He held up a half-finished quart of chocolate milk, saying that the *Garelick* [milk] man gave it to him this morning. He also had a carton of yogurt, and he said he'd be fine.

I offered him our gift cards together with another friend, Lee's, contribution to help him with whatever he needed. He took them gratefully, nodded his head and said, "Thanks! Tell Sue and Lee I said thanks!" I told him that I would and that Sue had offered to help him with new glasses if he would like her to. He was grateful, but he declined the offer, saying that he wasn't going to accept them from Mr. Margolis either – he'd let *MassHealth* [Medicaid] take care of the bill when the time came. He'd wait his turn. He said, "As long as I can see a red-tailed hawk, I'm OK." Pointing to the top of the building across the street, he said, "Those are seagulls." I looked and, indeed, they were. So, I said "OK," but if there was anything he needed, I told him that Sue asked me to tell him she would be glad to help him with it.

He was very grateful and said that he'd like to keep the option open. But "please tell Sue that if there is something that I need I will let you know. Really, I will let you know." I agreed and started to say good-bye, when he interrupted, "Oh, ya know, I haven't forgotten your slate … It's just that …" I finished his sentence for him: "… life's gotten really complicated lately." I told him I wasn't worried about when he finished it. A month or so ago he had told me about some of the work that he did painting pictures of light houses on small slabs of slate, in addition to the copper lanterns that he used to make. He used an old nail to etch the picture on the slate and then he would paint it in. Sue and I had "commissioned" him to make one for us, and we gave him a small down payment. We thought that we might help sell them for him on the South Shore and wanted to have him make a sample. Sue said that visitors to Cohasset have a thing for buying lighthouses. She used to own a card and gift shop in Cohasset center. Then I told him that Sue asked if she could help him with purchasing the paints. He deferred saying that a couple of years ago when he was making the slates, he was able to stock up and still had some left. So he thanked me again with a smile, and nodded his head.

Before I left he rummaged around in his back pack and produced another "coupon." "Here, I want Sue to have this, too."

I left with a smile and walked down the *Freedom Trail* to work.

September 14, 2006

Mr. Margolis was finishing up a conversation with Bob as I waited for the light at the corner of Park and Tremont. Bob was sitting on his crate with his legs covered with an open umbrella. Rain was predicted for the day and he was prepared. They both greeted me as I walked over. Mr. Margolis was sporting another cast-bound arm – this time the left one. I thought it was from the earlier run-in with his cat [or his wife – we never actually resolved that], but he said that, no, this was yet another one. As he was saying good-bye, he shared that his doctor told him he was "accident prone." He wished us well for the day, and as he walked down Tremont Street he said, "I told him I never have accidents when I'm prone." We both chuckled, and Bob clapped, saying, "That's a good one!"

Checking in with him, Bob said that he was better today, but his "blood pressure wasn't cooperating." I told him I found someone to help me with the camera and he replied, somewhat embarrassed, that he needed to borrow it back for a while as Mr. Davis, the gentleman who was doing the documentary, suggested that they have some still shots. I told him that I would be happy to bring it in next week to loan it back to him.

I told him that Sue wanted to come in with me to town sometime and meet him, and he said he'd love that. I also told him that my office was going to be moved off-site temporarily for the month of October. But, I assured him I would be back. He pouted and said, "I'll miss you!" I said that I felt badly about it and would miss our visits as well. He pulled out a cell phone that Mr. Davis had given to him, and said that when Mr. Davis brought him a new card for the phone, we could stay in touch that way for the time being. (Mr. Davis hasn't shown up for a while.)

He had mentioned that he liked to sing and, once in a great while, he would go to the services at the Park Street Church. I asked him if Sue and I might go with him some Sunday. He said that if he went it was to the evening service as he liked to be outside in the morning on Sunday to see all the kids and to get food and cigarette money and all. I didn't know if that was a "yes" or "no" and sensed it best to leave it at that.

Just then another man in a wide pin-striped suit stopped by and offered him a black quilted vest, saying that he had come by a week or so ago to try to drop it off. Bob briefly explained his illness was preventing him from coming out. "Blood pressure and all, you know." I thought this must have been one of the Thursday morning breakfast gentlemen, and decided to let them have some time together. I interrupted briefly and told Bob that I had to get to work, and I wouldn't be coming to Boston on Friday as I had a meeting out of town. But I'd look forward to seeing him soon. I gave him a two-dollar handshake and wished him a good day. "Have a good one, yourself!" he called out as I walked down the street to work.

September 19, 2006

Bob was taking a poll yesterday morning on his corner: "Good morning, Sunshine. Who 'ya voting for?" he asked me. Trying to anticipate his response, I cautiously shared my choice of candidate. I don't usually share this kind of information, but felt it was safe with him. "Deval's leading so far," he said. He thought Deval Patrick had the best chance of winning, and "this state sure needs a change." "I can't vote cause I'm homeless," he told me – which I never thought about. I told him that I would vote on his behalf. "Vote early and often!" he replied, explaining that that's what they say in Chicago. "Was it Mayor Daly?" he asked. He told me that once another gubernatorial contender, Christy Mihos, had walked down and greeted him on his corner once. (His office is just a block up the street near the State House. He had it set up so you could see him "hard at work" through the window.) Bob told him that he had always shopped at Mihos' convenience stores, *Christy's*, when he was in Florida. He said Mihos thought that was grand and gave him a $20 bill.

Bob also asked me to relate to Sue that there was something she could do for him after all: he was preparing for what he believed would be "a long and very cold winter." He could use a pair of very heavy, rugged pants and she could probably pick them up at an Army surplus store. "And she should come in [to Boston with me] sometime, too." I told him that I would, indeed, pass on his request.

He said he was still having trouble with his blood pressure, and showed me the meter and the readings it saved in its memory over the last several days. He needed to get his prescriptions filled. I asked if he'd seen his doctor, and he said she's only available Mondays from 9 to 12 to see him. Today was Tuesday. A couple of familiar folks passed by and said good morning to him as we talked – he didn't poll them, though. Having to leave and get to work, I wished him well and he again advised: "Vote early and often!"

During October, my office had been temporarily moved to Charlestown, which was on the Orange Line, so our floor of the building could be refurbished. It would not be practical to make the routine stop at Park Street each day. So Sue and I decided to purchase gift cards for four weeks' food expenses and give them to Bob in advance. We wanted to be consistent. We wanted to let him know we could be trusted.

I remembered how Bob told me about the first time after the fire when he was on Boston Common and asked someone for money to buy food. He said that the man had figuratively raked him over the coals for asking, saying that he should be ashamed of himself and that he should get a job like other people. Bob said that from that time on he would never ask anyone for anything. That's why he had the signs sitting next to him. If people wanted to come over and make a contribution, he would take it, but he would never ask again. [I thought about how hard and demeaning it had been for *me* to ask.] He told me that people asked him about the fire and he'd tell them – he didn't mind. And when he received something that he couldn't use, he shared it with another person in a similar situation. He didn't like the guys who just hung out on the corner and shook a paper cup at passers-by. I told him it bothered me, too. I had asked the guy in front of the *7-11* store once if I could get him a sandwich or something inside, and he declined. I have always been troubled about just tossing coins into a paper cup – there's no real investment, no connection, no engagement. Is that how to treat a neighbor?

October 25, 2006

It was good to get back to the Boston office. It was harder working offsite; I never felt settled. We were cut off from the rest of our colleagues, and we had to be more deliberate in connecting for meetings instead of just running into someone in the hall and taking care of business. But, it was a minor problem in the scheme of things.

It was good to see Bob again and deliver a few food cards. He had been in the hospital for two days having problems with his feet because of the diabetes. He told me matter-of-factly that most homeless folks don't have their toes because of frostbite, but that he was luckier than most. [Certainly a more sobering perspective on toes.]

Changing the subject he related how, years ago, he had participated in the "Maggie Valley Scavenger Hunt." I can't recall where he said it was, maybe Pennsylvania or Virginia. He had a motorcycle, a BMW, and he and his girlfriend entered the contest for $100. They found all 10 items on the list and won $2,000!

Just then, John, an employee at the Park Street Church came out and told Bob that someone had dropped off a bag for him inside the church. "Bob Wright. That's your name, right?" he asked. Bob nodded. John said he could pick it up anytime and Bob asked if he could store it for him as it was hard to carry everything around with him. John would oblige.

November 16, 2006

Today Bob said he wanted to write a book called "The Man I Never Knew" which would be a story for kids. It would be about his life as told by a family who let him stay with them for a while; he slept on the floor in their living room, I think he said. They took care of him by seeing that he had a place to stay. But he said they never really got to know him, not deep inside.

He said he had looked at his stack of writings again and commented, "Gee, these are pretty good." He had once shared some of them with me. They were captured on a well-used 8 ½ by 11 writing tablet. He said many had gotten lost or stolen, but he had a pretty big stack now. One entry was about his experience in a shelter during the winter. He wrote that he preferred staying in the subway or outside in the 29 degrees of February rather than stay there. I had given him a wire-bound writing notebook and encouraged him to keep writing and to share his story. Another entry he read to me. It was about the stars and planets, the moon and the sun, the universe and measurements and such, but I couldn't keep up with "the math."

An undated entry near the end of November, 2006

Bob began our conversation saying that, since he'd been "out here" (some 12 years or so), he's seen how people "adopt the homeless." While he didn't begrudge this for others, he said that no one had ever "adopted" him. He didn't like using the word "adopted." But he went on to say that this was until "Jonathan, Jonathan Margolis and people like you and Susan came along. I don't know how to put it into words, but I feel cared for. You tell Susan, too." I told him it was because he "counted" in this world just as much as anyone else and that we all – Mr. Margolis and Susan and I – wanted him to be cared for. I told him again how others had been kind to me during my difficult time over the past year and that I had wanted to return the "grace" by doing the same for someone else. I won't forget *patchwork time.*

He told me his room was small and "you could fly a kite in it," meaning that it was rather "breezy." This was the first time he mentioned anything about the place where he stayed. He said, "You know it's been real cold these last few nights." He told me that someone had given him some long underwear, but that he didn't need it as he'd been sleeping in the lined jeans (pointing to Sue's gift that he was wearing) for the last three days and nights. He said that they kept him extra warm. Every three days he'd wash them out in the tub.

I asked him if he were planning to go to any of the places in town where they were providing meals on Thanksgiving Day. He said that he would be "M.I.A." (missing in action). He didn't like having to go to them and he'd rather just be alone for the day. Sometimes I feel like that, too.

Then he said, "Hey, would you do me a favor?" Yes, I would. "Could you go over to Dunkin' Donuts and get me a cup of ice? Sometimes it helps," he said. "They usually charge me for it." I was glad to help out. I asked for a cup of ice which, for me, was free. I wanted to bring him something else from the store, but he said, "No, just the ice is fine. You're doing enough."

December 4, 2006

Today I was thinking that Bob wouldn't be at his usual place because it's Monday and it's raining and snowing at the same time. I was thinking about getting off at a stop a block closer to work. But, I thought about it again and felt compelled somehow to take a chance and see if he was there. I thought he might be hungry. I stopped at Park Street, and he *was* there. I was so glad to see him. He said he didn't want to come out today, but he was [indeed] hungry.

We complained about the sharp notes the Salvation Army trumpeter across the street was hitting, and he said he preferred the sound of just the small bells that they ring. I told him I liked the bells, too. He winked and said he heard bells every time he saw me. Anyway, I'm glad I had the food cards to give him, but I also asked him if I could get him anything, e.g., coffee or a bagel or whatever, for right now. He asked for a cup of ice again as he had before, again saying that chewing on it helps. So, I went across the street to Dunkin' Donuts. This time, they charged me 83 cents for it, but I didn't care if it helped Bob get through the morning. On my way back, I handed out some extra money Sue gave me to a couple of other fellows outside the store holding cups for donations. When I got back to Bob's spot outside the church, the Salvation Army "soldier" was now ringing a bell. It sounded so sweet amidst the falling snow. It was getting late, so we wished that each other would "Have a great day!" He said, "See you tomorrow."

Later that evening...

The hickory tree in my suburban front yard blocked the light of the nearly full moon perched in a star-studded sky, casting its stark silhouette on the first snow of the year. I wondered if Bob would be warm this night.

December 6, 2006

Today was very cold, especially for one sitting on a milk crate on the sidewalk outside Park Street Church in Boston. The radio announcer said the temperature was 26 degrees. Even bundled up in a down parka, with lined jeans and warm boots, the wind goes right through to the core. Bob was having trouble with his toes, in spite of socks and boots that were warmed with batteries. We looked up at the top of the building across the street to see that the hawk had been replaced by a seagull. How do *they* stay warm I always wonder?

Bob told me again about how many homeless folk didn't have toes because of frostbite. He said he could always tell the ones who had lost them by the way they walked. His problem with his feet today didn't have to do with frostbite; it was from the diabetes.

Mr. Margolis arrived just after me. He was wearing a storm coat, scarf and beret. He told Bob that he had taken the "T" to the Government Center stop yesterday as it was cold and snowing and he didn't think that Bob would be there (after Bob mentioned he was) on Monday, saying "You're *never* here on Mondays." I was glad I listened to the little voice inside telling me yesterday morning to get out at Park Street.

December 7, 2006

I met Mr. Jones today. I think he's one of the Thursday breakfast group regulars. There's a group of men – "influential Bostonians" or "movers and shakers" as Bob calls them – who get together for breakfast just up the street every Thursday. I can't just recall the name of the restaurant, but I'll go for a walk some day and check it out. I think he said it's a prayer breakfast of sorts. Bob had been invited to go from time to time, and the group would absorb the $20 fee for his breakfast. He said he was their "token" homeless person. He said they also had a token Black and a token Hispanic who had also been invited. Anyway, Mr. Jones was very generous to Bob and said goodbye with what I think was a "$20 handshake."

When Mr. Jones came, Bob was telling me about John, "…you know [imitating John's gruff voice and waving his arms] 'Can anyone give me a dollar for a cup of coffee?'" He said that he had gotten to know John at a rehabilitation shelter (I think he said it was the Sarah McGuinnes home) for homeless folks who had short-term health care needs. Bob had gone there "instead of [the alternative of] sleeping in a wheelchair outside Park Street Church" when he had broken his leg. He couldn't wait to leave the place. John was there as well, but Bob didn't know what he was "in for." I asked if he knew his story, but he didn't. He said, though, he had an addiction for buying lottery tickets, saying he hit it once for $5,000. Bob said after that he wasn't around for a week or so. But he reappeared clean-shaven and clean-clothed and back "to work" looking for handouts. He told me how a local radio station up the street had interviewed John one day and, in doing so, made fun of him and his wretched situation.

I told Bob that Sue had offered to buy him another pair of insulated jeans. He said that it would really be helpful. I would relay this to her.

Bob's neuropathetic toes were really hurting now and the doctors, he said, wanted to amputate some of them. Wanting to lighten up the subject, he said he was worried about how he would wear thongs in the summer if that happened to him. Relating the forthcoming frosty forecast for the evening, I asked if he had a warm place to stay tonight. He said he did.

December 8, 2006

As the Alewife-bound Red Line commuter train screeched to a halt and opened its doors at the North Quincy stop, an errant white feather, presumably from a passenger's well-worn down parka, danced mid-air in the train car amidst a flurry of glittering new snowflakes ushered in on the heels of an early December gust.

When I got off the train in Boston, I climbed the long stairway from the underground to the plaza above. I crossed Park Street but there was no sign of Bob. As I walked down Tremont Street in the blustery December morning wind, a herd of crackling-dry leaves sprinted on ahead of me just outside the Granary Burial Ground, scraping the sidewalk on their way. When I got to my office building, two poofy, plumped-up pigeons greeted me just outside. I don't know how they survive in this deep freeze, but that's something God takes care of. I'm glad Bob had a warm place to stay last night.

December 13, 2006

It was ironic. A jazzed-up version of "God Rest Ye, Merry Gentlemen" was being played by a lone saxophonist standing on the sidewalk just in front of the iron bars of the Old Granary Burial Ground. There rested, indeed, the remains of many sleeping souls. The tones of the sax were a haunting indictment with something of an "in-your-face" quality. Some days in the city it's hard to prevent the sinking desperation and helplessness that I feel when I see so many souls who have been left to wander these streets.

Bob wasn't there this morning or the last two mornings for that matter. I think he's having more trouble with his feet. Prayers for healing, "comfort and joy" for all these souls!

December 14, 2006

Another Thursday. If Bob was going to be at his post, this would be the day. And he was. I was grateful for the mild December weather. He was, too. The Thursday morning group members started passing by, most greeting him with a smile and saying, "I'll catch you on the way back."

He'd been out [or rather "in"] the whole week. He was, indeed, having trouble with his feet relating to me that he was up at 2 a.m. and gave himself an injection of insulin hoping that it would help the pain. He said it seemed to. I'm not sure if that's how it works [I know just enough about some things medical to get me in trouble], but even if he says it gives him relief, that's fine by me. He said again that he'd not been using the full dose in order to make it last longer. I can't imagine being cold, hungry and aching and having to sit outside on a milk crate in the cold hoping folks will drop a few coins into my cigar box on the sidewalk so that I might be able to eat tonight, or allow myself to use the full dose of insulin instead of feeling compelled to ration it. I can empathize to a degree, but I've never actually "worn his shoes" and felt the pain of aching, starving toes.

Changing the subject, he looked up at me and started, "Hey, would you mind ..." "Would you like some ice?" I interrupted him. "I brought you some." "What are you, psychic or something?" he said. I told him that I had put some in a plastic bag to keep my lunch cold and he was welcome to it. (Actually, I had packed bags of ice all week for him in case he had wanted some again. On the other days that he wasn't there, the ice stayed in my backpack and did, indeed, keep my sandwich and yogurt cold. When I ate my lunch, I thought about Bob eating just ice.) He popped the icy morsel into his mouth, asking if it was "gourmet ice." He said one of the biggest rip-offs was bottled water. But he was grateful for it.

I told him that I wouldn't be around on Friday as I had a meeting in Framingham. He shuddered and said that's where he had been living at the time of the fire. He hated Framingham and I thought it best to refrain from speaking about it for the time being. He shares his recollections every now and then, but I hadn't remembered where the fire was. I changed the subject and asked him again about his measurements for the jeans. "They're 36 by 32." I'll see if I can get the catalog number later on. Bob said to "say hi to Sue" as we shared a double-handed hand-shake good-bye.

December 19, 2006

On the train ride this morning I was remembering a commercial for the "Star Registry" that I heard on the radio while driving to the "T." They sell people the "right" to name a star after someone. I also remembered the impassioned discussion on NPR about the need for us to "win the war on terror." How ludicrous are both notions. Who gives us the right to "own the right" to name a star? How can you ever do away with evil?

Star Gazer Gazette

I think it sheer audacity to claim the right to sell a star!
It's an unabashed bamboozle, yet, I hate to think there are
true suckered souls who'll buy them just like they'd buy a car.
My sense is our humanity's gone just a bit too far!

And, take the "war on terror" [please!]. Have we lost all sense?
To think that we could win it is just impudent nonsense.
For as long as we will live on earth, dark and light dwell side by side,
an unremitting cycle from which none of us can hide.

But long ago one winter night, there rose the brightest star.
Three ancient philosophers gazed upon it from afar.
They set out on a journey, not knowing what they'd find,
but faithfully they sought the place over which the star did shine.

They found a tiny Savior, who was sleeping in a barn.
He was Immanuel – "God with us" – they would later learn.
He was born to heal all people, to show the way of peace.
He *is the light of all the world; through **Him** all war will cease.*

December 21, 2006

I pulled up the collar on my coat to ward off the strong December breeze that was blowing in through the open door of the subway car. People with backpacks and packages were posturing to hold their space as they started filling up the benches. One rather sporty looking, middle-aged man had a gym bag, an insulated lunch bag and a yellow plastic shopping bag of wrapped holiday gifts. He sat across from me on the end seat and was determined to take up one and a half seats-worth of space on the bench. His long legs sprawled outward, cradling his "stuff" on the floor space in front him, made it hard for anyone to sit next to him.

At one of the stops along the way, an Asian woman boarded all bundled up in a fuzzy, dark jade-green down jacket that made her displace twice as much space. She was determined to have a seat and wedged her way in to the half seat that was exposed between "sports-guy" and another passenger, one of the only seats left. Both of them sat with hunched up shoulders trying not to acknowledge the other. Another very large lady came on the train at the next stop and sat in the middle seat of the long bench upon which I sat. It was like a "wave" (or maybe I should call it a ripple, as it was not very enthusiastic) as she inserted herself. As each of us was affected by her presence, we shifted to the left and right of her to become more comfortable. As we continued on into the city, I realized it hadn't been the winter wind at all that was blowing in through the door. The air conditioning was on.

Bob was there today [Thursday again]. He'd been in a mighty blue "funk" and said he was depressed about the season and all. But we talked a bit and he seemed to perk up some. I handed him an envelope with a bunch of supermarket gift cards in it from Sue and me, as well as my sister. I had shown her the camera and she asked if she could buy it as she was wanting to buy a digital camera anyway. I suggested that she just make a donation to Bob. She did and I turned it into some more food gift cards. He was mighty pleased – he said he might not have much at Christmas, but at least he would be well fed. He was grateful. I asked if the coupons we were giving him each week were enough and he said, indeed, they were. He said that he didn't have anything left over at the end of the week, but he was frugal and spent the money wisely and made it last.

Next I asked him about a phone. He said Mr. Davis had shown up but only briefly as he was off again to handle his family affairs in the Midwest. Bob told him that he felt as though he were taking advantage of him. We talked more about getting a phone. He said that it would be really good if he could get some simple plan where you just add minutes. So, the phone is a go!

Finally, just before Mr. Margolis arrived, I had given Bob a copy of my book of song lyrics. I was trusting that this was the right thing to do. Maybe it will inspire him to get his own writings together … but that's not my call. Just as Mr. Margolis arrived, Bob pointed up to show us the red-tailed hawk soaring above. I greeted him and said that I would let the two of them talk as I had to get to work. Mr. Margolis, Bob and I then wished each other happy holidays, "such as they were," I said – meaning that I wanted to acknowledge we're in different places. Bob said, "See you tomorrow?!" I said that was a sure thing.

December 22, 2006

It was a breeze driving in to the Braintree "T" station today. Even though I left 10 minutes later than I normally do, I trusted the WBZ "Traffic on the 3's" report of "just a tap of the brakes at Union Street" – my destination. I arrived in just 20 minutes!

After finding a seat on the train and sitting down, I looked up only to be challenged: "Do you have what it takes to reprogram the entire airline industry … while it's running?" The ITA Software advertisement posted in the subway car clearly was not intended for me. No, indeed, I don't have what it takes to do that. I do other things.

The sun was just rising around 7:00 a.m. when we pulled out of the station to make the trip into the city. While I was facing west, a curious pink sky out the window in front of me encouraged me to turn around and look to the east. There were layer upon layer of sky-wide blue and pink "cotton candy" streaks that sat atop the railway cars on the horizon, a seemingly endless line. At the first stop, a crew-cutted, middle-aged man came in and sat across from me. He was wearing a long, medium grey, double breasted overcoat, jeans and black leather boots. He frequently looked skeptically from side to side as he sat down, but then invested himself in the Metro newspaper. But from time to time during the ride in, his eyes would dart back and forth checking things out.

At the next stop a young, white-blond woman came in wearing a bright red jacket and blue jeans and pulling a blue suitcase – very patriotic. She sat next to me. This being the Friday before the long holiday weekend, everyone seemed to be wearing jeans to work. So was I.

Bob wasn't there this morning as I thought he would be. He said, "See you tomorrow!?" yesterday; I said that he would. But, it was a cold morning and I'm hoping he had "earned" enough on Thursday so that he wouldn't have to go out again today. I was concerned that I didn't get to tell him that I was taking some time off from work during the Christmas holiday week. His needs don't stop; in fact, they're only enhanced when it's holiday time.

As I walked down Tremont Street on this cold December day, I passed a woman all bundled up pushing a shopping cart filled with all of her worldly possessions in the right lane down the street.

I pray for joy to the world.

January 2, 2007

The ride through the streets of my sleepy suburban town at 6:15 a.m. was somehow different today. It was still dark and there were white twinkly Christmas lights still draped around town; they seemed more peaceful and special now that the crazy rush of the holidays had come to an end. Today everyone was waking up to go back to school or work. As I continued down Route 123 toward Route 53, a huge, nearly full January moon sprang up through the trees over Jacob's Pond. A friend had tried to explain to me once that its size had to do with the layers of atmosphere through which it was viewed, or something like that. I can't remember. Anyway, it hung in the north sky and I followed it up Route 53 to Route 3 toward the Braintree "T" station. I felt like one of the magi following the star shining over Bethlehem, which, I remembered, according to the story, they would be doing just about now two millennia ago.

But the heavenly body I was following would take me just as far as Boston today.

A new month, a new year and a new Charlie Card for the ride on the "T." Sitting on the bench in the subway car, facing east toward the dawning January sky, a long blue-grey cloud stretched across it as far as the eye could see. It was underlined by a dark, rose-pink neon line.

I thought back on the week and about how two former presidents had died. One, from the United States of America, would be honored with a state funeral today; the other one, from Iraq, will be dishonored for all time. One died of natural causes, and one as a result of a poorly conceived government policy.

Bob wasn't there this morning. All I could see were the remnants of *First Night* ice sculptures melting into the Boston sidewalks.

January 3, 2007

The now-full moon was up a little higher in the sky this morning. I had left some 10 minutes later than yesterday, which, today, made a big difference in my drive time; and the subway car was really packed. An interesting phenomenon occurred – the free Metro newspaper that many folks read on the train had an insert for the Salter Institute which promised to "provide career training that really worked." The insert dropped from most of the papers onto the floor of the subway car. Lo and behold, no one picked them up. Amazing, just amazing.

It seemed like there were more travelers than usual, too, who were either getting on or off at South Station, going to or coming from a train or the airport. At one point I was face-to-face (face-to-torso, would be more accurate) with a pure black-and-white, medium-sized-hound's-tooth-plaid jacket, so well crafted – the plaids were so well matched – that you couldn't tell if it had a zippered front seam or not. (I got a really close look!) At Downtown Crossing I almost got clobbered with an overstuffed backpack that extended back well behind its bearer. The lady sitting next to me said the things should be "outlawed." Then a young fellow boarded with a hard-shell guitar case and suitcase; he appeared to be coming from an airport as his stuff had tags attached all over. I wanted to talk "guitar talk" with him, but decided not to strike up a conversation. I really wanted to just go home today and play my own guitar. As I exited the train at the Park Street stop, the loudspeaker announced that the next Red Line train to Braintree was arriving. Oh, that I could just board *that* train and go back home.

Emerging from the underground onto the plaza, the only things sitting in front of Park Street Church were some blue Boston Police Department saw horses that would be put up later today to block off Park Street – one of the routes to the State House. Former Governor Romney is scheduled to make his "lone walk" down the steps today at 11 a.m., so my sense is that Bob was laying low. In fact, none of the "regulars" were around. I think the Mayor wanted to "clean up" the riff-raff again, as he had done just before Christmas – swept them "all under the rug." A New England Cable News truck rounded the corner from Tremont onto Park, no doubt to secure an early position to cover the step walking later this morning.

January 4, 2007

There was just a fuzzy cotton ball of a moon in the northern sky this morning. It was overcast and unusually mild for January. It was a low-energy morning; I hadn't gotten as much sleep as I needed because I was out late last evening practicing with the "eclectic folk" trio that I'm in. Driving along in the car nursing a travel mug of coffee, the bridge of my nose hurt from where I whacked it with the music stand during practice. As I was setting it up last evening, it stuck as I tried to pull it up higher. All of a sudden the top part disengaged from the bottom and got me right between the eyes. How would I explain the black and blue to my workmates? What a klutz!

When I got to the top of the subway platform in Braintree, there were two trains idling and waiting to go. The train scheduled to go first was relatively full, even at the beginning of the line. As I thought about boarding it and squeezing into a seat, the bell sounded, signifying that the doors would be closing and the train would soon be off. Without missing a beat, I walked to the other side of the platform. I strode the full length of the empty, waiting train and took my time selecting a seat in the last car.

This time I sat facing the east so that I could just be quiet and watch the sun rise. As pink clouds transformed into salmon and then to coral, an immense swarm of black birds practiced their maneuvers, perfectly synchronized as they flew to and fro and to again. When it was time for the train to start on its journey into town, they had all perched atop the massive cinder-blocked "T" entryway structure, which actually formed an "H" at the top.

I didn't think Bob would be there today. It was inauguration day for our new governor, and there were police and barriers everywhere blocking off Park Street. But, to my [pleasant] surprise, he was there. I hadn't prepared my offering. So at the top of the stairs, but still inside the entryway, I fished around in my purse for the supermarket gift cards for him for the week. I had also wanted to share a Dunkin' Donuts gift card with him. So I put them in my pocket and went out to greet him. He looked surprised and happy to see me. We shook hands and started to talk. He told me an off-color story and, quoting a friend of mine, I told him, "I could have gone all day without hearing that!" He snickered.

He said he was afraid of catching cold so he was taking precautions wearing a heavy jacket and scarf. He couldn't afford to get sick. I asked if he had been OK last week, and told him I hadn't had a chance to let him know that I was taking the week off from work. He came out only one day that week he said. Thursdays are the days that he would make himself go out because of the Thursday morning group. He could count on them to help out. He had run out of food and cigarettes again today, and it was Thursday. I gave him the food coupons and offered him the Dunkin' Donuts card. He said he'd love a cup of coffee. I offered to do the errand for him just across the street, and he said you use the card for the coffee. And could I get him a cup of ice as well. I could, and did. They didn't charge me for it this time.

I came back with the coffee and then needed to be on my way to work. I was glad to see him. After I left, I kept thinking all day if and why he had to remain "Bob, Homeless by Fire."

January 8, 2007

The black-and-white hound's tooth pattern of last week was repeated today. First, in a collapsible umbrella, carried onto the subway car somewhere along the way by a rather large woman in black pants, black patent-leather looking clogs and an apple-green wool coat. Her hair was black, short and spiky, except for a white patch in front which looked like it was intentionally "processed" to match the pattern in her umbrella. She was carrying a large, fanciful brown leather handbag which she placed on the floor. There were leather roses, rosebuds and leaves fashioned out of the same leather hanging all around it. The second hound's tooth pattern appeared as I passed Talbot's on School Street. I had been window shopping and happened to notice two such upholstered chairs just inside the front door. I don't think there's much significance to this repeating pattern stuff, only that it illustrates the notion that [in my experience] when one is pregnant all you see are other pregnant ladies. When you're not, one doesn't tend to see them as much. ["Let them eat cake" comes to mind.]

Bob wasn't there today. It's raining, it's Monday – a sure bet.

As I unbundled my tote bag in my office, I thought about the passage in *James* that I read this morning that admonished its readers against showing partiality toward people with means. I thought about how our new governor opened up all of the usually invitation-only inauguration events to anyone who wanted to attend last week. He said that everyone was welcome in the State House, because it belonged to them. It felt good to be at work today.

January 11, 2007

Now, I understand. There's a reason that, as children, we learn to play games. It's so we can use the skills, for example, that we learned when playing "Musical Chairs" now as adults when sauntering down the line of waiting subway train cars to see how far we can get until the bell rings and evokes the reaction (in that predictable, Pavlovian knee-jerk, count-on-the-stimulus-begetting-a-reaction kind of way) that "you'd better find a seat fast because the doors are going to close and this train is going to be out of here!"

As soon as we embarked, the overhead speaker on the subway car announced, "Next stop, Park Street. Change here for the Green Line." I smiled and thought, "Hmmm, what a short trip!" It's always amusing when the announcements get mixed up like that. But, for someone who's new to the area, I suppose it can be quite confusing.

Another childhood lesson comes to mind: "Stay within the lines." I wish that the 60-something, "blond" paged-boyed woman, wearing a tailored white wool coat, black scarf and sequined wool hat with bag to match, who parked herself next to me had learned that lesson. She also wore chipped black nail polish, which seemed inconsistent. Anyway, she simultaneously flicked open her *Metro* and jutted her elbows back, claiming her "personal space," which included part of my left side. Without an apology, or even an acknowledgment that she had made contact, she went on to read her paper. Staying "within the lines" I readjusted my tote bag so as to protect myself from further attack. She obviously had not learned the fine art of newspaper un-folding and page-turning while riding on a common carrier. She was clearly out of, and over the, line!

Although I was sitting facing the west, I noticed the sun was glaring in my eyes. The newly risen sun was reflecting so brightly in the window that I wondered for a minute if I had chosen the wrong side of the train. But soon we were underground and almost to Park Street.

Thursday, but no sign of Bob. It's 19 degrees this morning and I can't say as I blame him. I hope he'll be there tomorrow.

January 12, 2007

All morning I thought it was the 13th – Friday the 13th. But, to my surprise, it's not! I'm a little more sleep-deprived this week than I thought! I'm not superstitious or anything and, anyway, there are a lot of "13's" in my life that have positive associations. My house is number 13, and my son and I moved there when he was 13, and it's a wonderful place.

Anyway, it is, indeed, a Friday. There were more blue-jeaned passengers, including me, on the "T" today. Maybe that's why the young businessman in a suit and black wool overcoat who sat next to me stood out all the more. *He* knew how to read a paper on a cramped train. He had the full-cut *Boston Globe* but managed to stay "within the lines." Black-and-white hound's tooth repeated again today – this time in a very large, distorted print on a young woman's cap. (And, now that I think of it, it repeated again in a smaller, finer print in the suit jacket of a friend I was with at a meeting earlier this week. Still not sure why I find this so interesting ...)

It was dark and overcast this morning, and as we rode along, a phantom-like train on the parallel commuter rail track shadowed us for a while and then passed on by. I thought to myself that I may be riding the "Phantom Train" someday as soon as the connection is completed in Scituate, the town next to mine. As it sped past, instead of a caboose at the end, there was an engine – I wonder if they still call them locomotives [which, now that I look at that word, I suppose could be interpreted as "mad intentions"] – pushing the train backwards. What a chuckle!

It was milder today – well, that's relative I guess. It was 19 degrees yesterday, and today it was 46. Anyway, I hoped that I'd see Bob, and as I came up from the underground, there he was, finishing a conversation with a "regular." As I crossed the street, the fellow left. Then, as I approached Bob, Mr. Margolis appeared at the same time. We all greeted each other, and Bob also said, "How's Sue?" I assured him that Sue was fine. But, as I usually like to let them talk together privately, I felt a little awkward lingering. But, I stayed just as a presence I guess. "Showing up is 90 percent of life" as the saying goes.

Bob was shaking in spite of being bundled up in a down parka, scarf and so on. Mr. Margolis asked him if it was from the cold or from the diabetes. Bob assured him it was from the cold and he just couldn't "shake it" [interesting term he used]. Bob said his heart was acting up again, too. Then Mr. Margolis asked Bob if he had his [nitroglycerine] patches. No, Bob was out of them. He asked if Bob had seen his doctor this week. No, and this Monday was a holiday so he couldn't go then either. Could he get over to Mass General to get his prescription filled? No, as they hold your prescription "hostage" until you give them the co-pay. "Then, let's go get some right now – at CVS," said Mr. Margolis. "Do you have your prescription with you?" Bob fished around in his bag and pulled out a pack of papers that were from his numerous prescriptions. He was reluctant as he'd still have to provide a co-payment. That didn't matter to Mr. Margolis; he would take care of that. Bob still didn't want to go. I think it's a combination of wanting to collect as much as he can from the regular commuters as well as not wanting to accept any more help from Mr. Margolis; he was very generous. Mr. Margolis told him that if he didn't want to go now, and if he didn't have the money for the co-pay, to just go to the pharmacy when he was finished here and give him a call and he'd come down and take care of it. Bob reluctantly agreed.

It was time to go, and I gave Bob the food gift cards. Mr. Margolis remarked that he "didn't know that plastic could be so nourishing!" to which Bob commented that he'd been living on it all week. He talked about his unfortunate experience trying to obtain food stamps in the past. He thought he might try again, but the problem was that he didn't know how to use them. When he had applied for the stamps before, he had, in all seriousness, asked the woman at the "state agency of whatever" how to use them, and she said, sarcastically and unhelpfully, that he could just "take them outside to the [human vultures] lurking outside the building and sell them for 60 cents on the dollar." Boy is she in the wrong business.

Over time, during the course of our conversations, I learned that Bob's room was in Revere near the beach; he referred to it as a small box. "Is it warm where you stay, Bob?" I asked as this had been a concern of mine for some time. Somehow I couldn't be comfortable in my own home thinking about him shivering and in want. "Yes," he said. It was a "furnace." He lived on the first floor of an old building and the heat blasted through the grate. He said he tried putting a slate on it to stop it from pouring in. We all agreed that life seemed to come in extremes. Mr. Margolis asked him if he had a social worker. No, he didn't. We encouraged him to ask about that when he went to the hospital to see his doctor.

Mr. Margolis told Bob that he had to get to work, but encouraged him again to call. Then, he said to me, with a nod of his head in the direction of Government Center, "You walking this way?" Yes, I was. So we both waved good-bye to Bob and wished our friend well. We walked down Tremont Street for a block. I asked him how long he had known him, and he said he'd seen him around for three years or so. We both agreed that helping Bob allowed us to do our part to help people. I commented that Bob made it easy to do so, and we agreed that he was a "really good guy." Mr. Margolis said that he'd see about resurrecting an inquiry that he had previously made on Bob's behalf about a shelter that was for disabled homeless folks. He thought Bob was on their waiting list; he'd look into it. I told him I wished I could do more for Bob, and he said that I shouldn't discount what I was doing. Just showing up, being friendly and talking with him was enough. He asked me what I did for work and I told him about the obesity prevention program and how it still seems such a strange juxtaposition to my experience knowing Bob and encountering the other Park Street Angels every day. Bob said that maybe the people the program is trying to help should meet him. Maybe it might change their way of thinking about what they have. Maybe …

It was time for me to turn right at School Street. We wished each other a good weekend. Today – un-Friday the 13th – felt lucky somehow.

January 16, 2007

They're predicting a very cold snap this week. Later today the mercury will start its descent, so I packed extra mittens and stuff in my bag. When I left home this morning the temperature was somewhere around 40 degrees and the rain storm that had awakened me at 1:30 a.m. was moving on. We were warned that in the storm's wake a meteorological vacuum would be created, which would draw in frigid Arctic air later tonight. I remembered that 25 years ago this day, at this very time of day, there was a snow storm. At this time 25 years ago I was in labor. My son was born close to 8:30 a.m. on January 16th, 1982 – my actual due date. I laugh when I think about how obliging I was to be on time! (Or was it *he* who was being punctual?!) I hope to see the birthday boy sometime this week to mark his quarter-century achievement!

My backpack was very heavy today. In addition to my regular "stuff" was a notebook of work that I had taken home over the weekend. There was no room in it for Bob's new lined jeans, so I just carried them outside. No matter; I needed more "weight-bearing exercise" anyway.

In the parking lot at the Braintree "T" I found a pair of ear muffs. Wishing that I could get them back to their rightful owner, I owned that that was a probable improbability. So, I picked them up and put them in the outside pocket of my pack. I would bring them to Bob.

Riding the train this morning I couldn't stop thinking about how a 15-year-old boy was killed over the weekend. Arriving from Providence, Rhode Island, where his step mother put him on the train back home to Easton, Massachusetts, he stepped off the train, waved to his mother who was waiting for him in the parking lot, took the shortest route to her, which was over the fence and across tracks. He was struck by a non-stopping Acella train tearing down the tracks at over 100 miles an hour. He died instantly. I think every mother's heart was shattered when they heard of the tragedy. I know mine did and still does when I think about it. I can identify with the mother, being a single mother myself who, a decade ago, made the same type of arrangements for my son to be with his dad and step family, meeting at a halfway point between our two homes. But I can't begin to understand the horror of witnessing such a tragic accident and loss of a child.

Bob wasn't there this morning. I'll probably not see him until the end of the week.

January 18, 2007

A familiar-looking, casually dressed man boarded the idling subway car just after I took my seat. I couldn't quite place him and as we rode along I kept trying to think of where I saw him before. Then it hit me: "Leo McGarry!" [*West Wing*] I commented to myself. He looks just like "Leo McGarry!" But it was hard to make the connection as he wasn't in a suit – and I recall his character always wore a suit. I'd become something of a West Wing junkie of late. I never watched it on TV, as I don't really watch TV much. But my sister introduced it to me on DVD. It's entertaining as well as educational – and so clever. I love clever!

Anyway, I suppose my commute this morning could have been worse. I suppose I could have been on the disabled train in front of us that probably had to kick everyone off and then limp along to be fixed while the off-put passengers would have to wait for another train in the freezing cold. [Later, I learned that a friend who lived in North Quincy had been on the disabled train in front of me and was among those who were, indeed, kicked off to wait in the bitter cold for the next one. He said they were packed in on the platform so tightly that if anybody moved, they'd fall onto the tracks.]

While I've been trying to be "thankful in all things," this would put my resolution to the test! I was aching from forgetfully, stupidly lifting something heavy yesterday. In doing so, a usually non-troublesome, formerly herniated disc had been incited. I was waiting, hoping that the Advil would kick in soon. I was also anticipating a very challenging meeting at work this morning. I was carrying an LCD projector from a presentation the day before back in to work. And, since I didn't want to annoy my sciatic nerve any more than necessary, I left out a lot of stuff that I usually carried in my bag. I decided to leave the second pair of lined jeans that Sue ordered for Bob at home, rationalizing that he wouldn't be there today because of the bitter cold, and that I really did need to take care of myself. I'd lugged them in Monday and Tuesday hoping that he'd be there, but he hadn't shown up all week. Anyway, in the spirit of being thankful, I was grateful that I had a seat on the train and that I was warm, that I had come from a warm, comfortable home where I had had a luxuriously wonderful cup of coffee, that I had clothes to keep me warm and a heated car to get me to the train station, and that I had a job to go to in the first place that allowed all that. My heart is grateful.

Anyway, we idled interminably between the Quincy Center and Wollaston stops [OK, it was half an hour]. When we were finally underway and arrived at the Wollaston stop, we picked up a cattle car's worth of rosy-cheeked passengers shivering on the platform. When we made our approach to the next stop, North Quincy, there was an impassioned shriek over the loudspeaker: "Bikes! No bikes on the train! The train's too full! No Bikes!" We were, indeed, packed in like cattle. I am also learning about boundaries and detachment as well, so I didn't say anything [but really wanted to] to the woman immediately in front of me whose poofy Prima-something black mittens hung precariously out of her down coat pocket ready to drop at a moment's notice. [Hmm …

does that mean that if I glanced at them for a split second, that's all it would take to make them drop? I never thought about that phrase before.]

Moving on ... after I got off the train at Park Street and walked up the stairs to the first level, schlepping my tote bag and the projector case over my shoulders, I wondered if I would make it through the "meat-grinder" turnstile. I did, but not without some precarious manipulations. I chose to take the escalator up the next flight, and as I approached the top kept saying to myself as if to Bob, "Don't be there, don't be there, don't be there." I was, after all worrying about him freezing there in the cold, as well as feeling not a little bit guilty considering my own comfort and not bringing his new pair of insulated jeans. Well ... he was there. Feeling like I let him down, I think I said "Oh, no" under my breath, which escaped in a white cloud as I walked out into the skimpy 12 degrees of heat. But something was different; he wasn't sitting on his crate but on the concrete sidewalk with his back up against the church. I couldn't believe it.

As I approached him, he said, "Good morning, Sunshine!" I smiled and said, "What are you doing here?!" I didn't mean it in a scolding way, but with more of an "I'm-so-concerned-about-you-being-out-in-this-frigid-cold-weather" sort of sentiment. We exchanged a warming two-handed handshake. "I've got to make rent," he said. I forgot the pain in my back and in my leg. I asked him how his feet were. "Oh, they're gone!" he said matter-of-factly. He removed the green-army-camouflaged-printed poncho that doubled now as a blanket covering his legs and, to my relief, I saw that he was wearing some rugged, lined work boots and some insulated warm-up pants. Then, pointing to the window in the church just above him, he said, "John – his office is right up there – is getting me some batteries." Someone had given him some battery-operated hunting socks, and John was one of his friends who kind of watched out for him. He could literally keep an eye on him out his office window when Bob was on the corner.

I gave him the cash that I had set aside to purchase his food gift cards, apologizing that I hadn't had time to buy them during the week. He said that it was better this time as he could use it to take care of part of the co-payment he'd need to get his prescriptions filled. He was going to the hospital pharmacy today, and had all of his pill bottles with him in a plastic bag. I asked him how long he would stay on the corner. "Nine o'clock," he said.

I asked him about his writing and if he had a chance to look at it while he was waiting out this long winter. I told him that he had taught me so much and that other people needed to hear his story. Would that be OK with him? He said he wouldn't mind if people learned of his story through his writings, but that he hadn't thought about them much recently. He thanked me for reminding him. He asked, "How's Sue?" I told him that Sue was in Florida with a close friend. They shared a love for painting I told him. He asked, "What kind?" "Watercolors, I think."

A woman, another regular, carrying a Tupperware container of cupcakes came by and said, "Bob, where's your crate?" "Oh, they confiscated it," he replied. It made me shiver to see him sitting there on the concrete sidewalk. "I'll be back with some chicken," she said. He acknowledged her promise, and she walked on quickly in the cold. She was going to the daycare facility.

He said he was going to take up a new job. He said that he once learned in school that no two snowflakes were alike. Jokingly, he said he was going to start designing new snowflakes. But then, with a twinkle in his eye, he admitted the work was only seasonal and that he wasn't sure what he'd do in the summer.

Just then, a large man and a small boy appeared. "Here are your batteries, Bob!" said the child with a beaming smile on his face. He was delighted with himself, and well he should be! He was showing kindness and concern. Bob introduced me to John, the boy's father, who was also holding a super-huge mug of freshly brewed and steaming tea. Bob asked the boy to take the gulp or so of cold coffee left in his Styrofoam Dunkin' Donuts cup and pour it out into the street. He would replace it with the steaming tea. He didn't want to use the ceramic mug. John tossed a couple of packets of sugar in Bob's cigar box and wished him well. He had to get his son off to daycare. Bob was grateful, both for the batteries that would bring his feet back to life and the tea that would warm him inside.

I said it was time for me to get to work – in fact, I was forty minutes later to work today because of the breakdown. But, I had to stay and just be with Bob for a while this morning. Someone explained it recently as "companioning."

January 19, 2007

The upstairs/downstairs commuter train rushed past us at what must have been twice our speed as we clickity-clacked along the MBTA track. As I looked in the illuminated train cars speeding by, I saw that some people were facing forward, some were looking backward. It occurred to me that I, on the other hand, was going sideways, with one eye, in its periphery, looking forward and the other looking back – on other trips this would, of course, alternate depending on which side of the train I was sitting.

Across from me sat two obese women, one on either side of the door on the end seats. I remembered the *NPR Story Board* interview that I heard this morning on the way in. A niece was interviewing her aunt who had grown up as an obese child, weighing 13 pounds at birth, 100 pounds when she was six and 250 when she was 10 years old. She spoke of how the kids used to make fun of her in elementary school; she was always self-conscious. But somehow she grew up and had a successful career as a teacher which spanned some three decades. She was asked her most important lesson; it was to use wisdom in all you do.

I felt compassion for her as I remembered being on the "chunky" side myself growing up. I was teased by my classmates; I was [as many of us were] taught the admonition, "Sticks and stones can break my bones, but names will never hurt me." Well, experience and wisdom tell me that that's just a big lie. Bullying through name calling *does* hurt one's spirit.

I wonder if any of the work that I'm involved in is making any kind of a difference. I felt sorry for the two women on the train.

I don't want to give [too much] time or energy in noting how an Asian man in an "obese" parka sat down next to me and was clearly "over the line." It's Friday and I'm tired and he annoyed me. But, wanting to be thankful in all things, it's Friday, I have one more day at work this week [a.k.a., I have a job to go to!] and then I can relax this evening. Over the weekend, hopefully, I'm looking forward to having a meal with my son to celebrate his birthday. There's a gift!

January 24, 2007

It's hard to get up and out the door on time on these cold January mornings. Sometimes leaving 10 minutes later, which is what I've been doing of late, means that the subway cars are apt to be packed. We were jammed in again this morning as the train picked up its last suburban passengers before going over the Neponset River into Boston. A twenty-something young man dressed in black slacks and a tailored grey wool coat, clinging to the vertical chrome bar in front of me by a black, wool-mittened left hand, held in his un-mittened right hand a Bruins hockey team travel mug full of coffee. I assumed it was coffee, as some of it pooled precariously in the top of the mug that he held at about a 30-degree angle. Without saying anything to him [I'm still practicing boundaries] I wondered all the way in whose leg it would drip on first, mine or the gentleman sitting next to me. Well, luckily the thought transference worked, for after several more stops along the way he looked down and held it upright.

It's Sue's birthday today and, as I recall, according to Native American culture it's customary for the one who has the birthday to give presents to the guests who come to celebrate the birthday with him or her. I'm told that's the true meaning of the term, "Indian giver." So I was finally able to give her gift of the second pair of lined jeans to Bob. He was thrilled.

He also said that he was honored to have been given the book of song lyrics that I had given him at Christmastime. He said, "all due respect" that he didn't subscribe much to the "religious" parts of it, but that he loved it and he said I had a true gift and that I should keep it up. He said that Mr. Margolis had just stopped by earlier [timing is everything!] and he had wanted to share the book with him, but he wanted to ask me first. I told him I'd be fine with that, and that it was his to do with as he pleased. I encouraged him to keep writing himself. He fretted that he didn't have the wherewithal to do it right now, that he was in a chronic "traumatic time" and he didn't have whatever it is that you need to sit with your writing and edit it and rework it. I told him I totally understood that, but to not give up on it in any case.

January 25, 2007

I've been "chewing" on a meeting that took place yesterday since I woke up this morning. I had denied – an old habit of mine – that my integrity during the discussion had been challenged; but it had been. Metaphorically, my approach to handling a certain situation that had come up at work was to "take the high road" and "turn the other cheek," but for this I had been [at least I felt] challenged. But I don't do well responding "on my feet," and I didn't advocate on my own behalf.

I remember a minister once explaining that it's important to understand the *context* – in this case the time in history and culture – in which such phrases as "turn the other cheek," "walk the extra mile" and "if someone demands the shirt off your back, give him your coat as well" were first spoken. Our contemporary [and apparently erroneous] adaptations and interpretations of such phrases suggest that they are tantamount to offering oneself as a doormat. But *Wikipedia* confirmed the minister's admonition:

> "...striking someone deemed to be of a lower class with the back of the [right] hand was used to assert authority and dominance. If the persecuted person 'turned the other cheek,' the discipliner was faced with a dilemma. The left hand was used for unclean purposes, so a back-handed strike on the opposite cheek would not be performed. The alternative would be a slap with the open [right] hand as a challenge or to punch the person, but this was seen as a statement of equality. Thus, they argue, by turning the other cheek the persecuted was in effect demanding equality.

> "Further ...by handing over one's cloak in addition to one's tunic, the debtor has essentially given the shirt off their back, a situation directly forbidden by Jewish Law. By giving the lender the cloak as well, the debtor was reduced to nakedness. Public nudity was viewed as bringing shame on the viewer, not the naked..."

Brilliant! But, all of this makes me think about how people misinterpret things from the *Bible* – things that were written in ancient times within ancient contexts and cultures and applying them to today. How ignorant *can* we be?

I'm praying for the right words to say, and to get rid of this anger. I'm also feeling guilty that I didn't have anything for Bob today. Surprisingly, he was there. Yesterday I had given him the cash instead of the gift card, the ear muffs that I had picked up at the Braintree "T" station parking lot, an extra disposable camera that I had received for a stocking stuffer, together with Sue's donation of new jeans. He was wearing them and said he had [gratefully] slept in them last night. I just feel frustrated at his situation, but I have to also remember that detachment is important. I also have to detach from this issue at work.

January 26, 2007

Today was the coldest morning that I could remember in a long time. It was one of those mornings that I had thought about last winter while at home, knowing that I would have to face going out into the sub-zero, wind-chilly Arctic air sooner or later when I got a full time job.

It was challenging for the waiting subway car to keep its passengers warm. The heat was blowing at full force inside in an attempt to compete with the 2 degrees of "heat" outside, which was reinforced by the 15- to 20-mile-an-hour wind gusts. Outside won. Sitting there on the bench, I could see my breath. I hoped that my feet would warm up in my wool-knee-sock-lined *Merrils*.

A very young, sandy haired urban professional in a long black wool coat and khaki slacks entered the car and took his seat at the end of the bench across from me. There was a man sitting next to him a seat's worth away, and he made the comment, in something like a Southern accent, that there were "six days of January left and it's finally here." Then I heard something about North Carolina. The man next to him offered a general acknowledgment to his friendly but apparently annoying [to him] chatter with an insincere smile; he quickly got out a pen and became involved in the daily *Sudoku* puzzle. I suspected the young gentleman was new in town.

He was not only new in town, but new to commuting on the MBTA. After his brief encounter with the soppy, sour-faced commuter on his end of the train, he staked out his territory on the floor in front of him, which an experienced rider knows is a big mistake. (I don't even want to think about it from a public health perspective.) It was indeed an accident waiting to happen. In front of him he placed his medium-sized Styrofoam cup of Dunkin' Donuts coffee and bag of whatever was in the bag for breakfast. He got out his paper and started reading it, reaching down from time to time to pull something out of the bag on which to munch or take a sip of coffee. I knew, I *just knew*…

Oh, well, at the next stop, in charged some freeze-dried souls. One was a woman about 5 feet 6 inches tall and close to 300 pounds; she had her eye on the seat next to me. I happened to catch her glance and made a half-hearted smile acknowledging where she was headed. Then I flexed my gluteus maximi, sat up tall and tried to take up only three-quarters of my seat. She sat down and I was pinned in for the duration. No matter; at least I was warmer.

Looking back from time to time to see how the young traveler was doing, I saw that he had gotten up quickly as a similar passenger sat down next to him on his end of the bench. He was either being a gentleman, giving up his seat to an older woman, or he was a quicker thinker than I was, and determined not to be pinned in. I think it was probably a bit of both, as she took up half of his seat along with hers. Anyway, I could see him between the other standees. He was now in front of the door holding his coffee cup in one hand and shaking drips of coffee from his cell phone with the other. He wanted this to be just a minor incident; he appeared to be looking around to see if anyone [hoping that no one] saw what happened.

As we picked up yet more passengers on the way, I came back to my own thoughts and was noticing the huge, square, flat red stone in the ring of the lady next to me. She was wearing a full-length, fur-trimmed black coat and a large black turban affair covering all of her hair except for one dyed-red curl that stuck out and arched upward on the side. She was speaking too, but not to anyone in particular.

After a while, I looked back over at the young gentleman, and I didn't know whether to feel utter pity for him or laugh. As any seasoned rider could have predicted, his coffee now had spilled all over the floor and he was sopping it up with his newspaper in a slapstick comedy sort of fashion. I don't know why his situation pulled so at my heart; I felt such pity for him that he didn't know what was coming. I felt sad for him that he had tried so hard to be friendly to people only to come up against a bunch of sour-pussed New Englanders. I pitied his innocence. It felt familiar.

It was a good choice today to take the Green Line and go one more stop to Government Center, which was only two blocks from my building. Bob said he wouldn't come out in the cold today, so I wouldn't chance missing him. As I emerged onto Government Center Plaza, the northwest wind was at my back. Had I gotten out at Park Street, I would have been walking head-on into the minus 14-degree wind chill. Pragmatism prevailed.

January 29, 2007

The psychology of subway seat selection I find to be fascinating; this behavior is so predictable. With the ten-seater benches on the train cars, passengers sit on the two ends first – never the middle – leaving eight seats left. As passengers board along the way, they sit so that there's a space between them and the next passenger. But at one point, there are two remaining seats together that people always have trouble negotiating – which one to choose? When they finally do sit down, however, they seem to be "of two minds," straddling the two seats that remain while leaving a little space between themselves and the passengers on either side. But, then, ultimately the decision is made for them by a newly boarded passenger claiming his/her individual, inalienable rights by wedging their way in that half space on one side or the other so that the former, more ambivalent passenger of the two withdraws to his heretofore allotted place. There's a lesson there, I think.

I'm glad Bob wasn't there this morning. It's a cold 29 degrees in Boston today.

January 30, 2007

I remembered a tune this morning that I was working on a few weeks, or maybe a month or so, ago around the holidays. At that time I remembered wanting to give some dedicated attention to the crafting of the words, but since I couldn't create enough quiet space then, I hummed the tune into my cassette tape recorder to save it for whenever I could find that space. From time to time I'd just play the chords and hum the tune during a practice so that I could "plant" it in my mind, but there were no words then.

But the tune was demanding my attention this morning on the ride in to Boston. The words, "Did you ever wonder if life is something more …" were "sketched" in my mind. It's a place to start.

January 31, 2007

It never fails; there's always an "outlier." A young man entered the train car and, instead of choosing to start the row on either end, he sat down right in the middle of the 10-seater bench across from me. Well, maybe not exactly in the middle; he'd have to sit either on seat number five or six.

At one stop, the train picked up two young women who looked like twins, or at least sisters. They were petite and athletic looking with sporty warm-ups and all. They stood right in front of me as I sat on the end seat. One read a paperback, and the other was working on a crossword puzzle in a newspaper. Neither one held on to anything. Maybe they were, indeed, gymnasts and had the strength and coordination not to have to. As the train bounced and swerved, their bodies flowed along with the train's motions like synchronized swimmers – simultaneously leaning a bit left, then back; up and down.

Bob was in his spot this morning and Mr. Margolis had just arrived. We made our usual greetings and remarked at how cold it was that day. Mr. Margolis advised, "Get used to it, my dear." Bob said he had cabin fever on Friday, a day where the temperature was in the very single digits with a brisk wind chill. He had ventured out some that day just around his place near Revere Beach, saying that all his life he seemed to "go into the eye of the hurricane," which, as Mr. Margolis explained, was really a calm place, but we understood Bob's meaning. Bob said he always seemed to be drawn into a crisis or chaos.

After Mr. Margolis and I wished him well, we walked down toward Government Center and brought up the possibility of checking out the Council for Elder Homeless on Bob's behalf – perhaps we could get his name on the waiting list. Just like me, Mr. Margolis said he sometimes gets involved in work and forgets about following up with things like this. I told him that Sue and I were willing to work with him – kind of like a team – to see if we could find a comfortable place or situation for Bob. We need to keep working on that one.

February 1, 2007

The whole city was a-buzz this morning with Ted Turner's "guerilla marketing" hoax to promote a stupid adult cartoon show – well, that is, a stupid cartoon show. What was he thinking!?

It was hard going to work today ... it's fraught with that chaos that Bob was talking about a few days earlier. But I know there's something that I'm supposed to be doing and learning there. Just not sure what that is yet.

Bob was giving out five-dollar Starbucks coupons, which had hand warmers attached to them, to his Angel peers. There was a guy hanging around the side of the Park Street "T" entrance – not just outside the entrance so that the un-needy might get miffed if he didn't give them one, but around the side where he could see folks and be more selective. Leave it to Bob to offer to help him out! Bob spoke of the fire in the Salem boat yard the day before and he was worried for Mr. Margolis. Mr. Margolis actually wintered his boat there; he said there was only some minor damage.

Bob was going shopping today and will plan to stay in tomorrow as cold temperatures along with a mixture of snow and rain are predicted. Mr. Margolis took extra care in warning him about the arctic cold that was due in next week. On a warmer note, we discussed the origins of Punxsutawney Phil's involvement with Ground Hog Day. According to Bob, it seems he came out of hibernation just to look for a date – just a one-night stand, mind you – and then back he would go into his burrow for a few more weeks and then a litter of baby groundhogs would be born into more temperate spring weather. The result is that, no matter fact or fiction, after February 2nd we all agreed that there are always six more weeks of winter.

February 2, 2007

I'm feeling rather "Andy Rooney-ish" today…

I think it's fair to say, indeed, with every intention of making a pun, that obesity is an expanding, and I dare say exploited, growth market. If "necessity is the mother of invention," there'll be no end to the variety of super-sized things that are being, and will need to be made! Why just this summer a new line of larger child car seats hit the market for "at risk for overweight" and "overweight" toddlers. (We can't call them overweight or obese yet; it appears that would be "name-calling.") But, it's only a matter of time before subway train manufacturers produce broader-based seats to accommodate only eight or nine broader-butted passengers per bench. Or maybe they'll make larger train cars to accommodate the super-sized seats so they can maintain 10 butts per bench (measured in BPB's). Right now it's just so pathetic to see everyone smushed in together. No civilized society should allow it. On a brighter, economic note, just think of what this means, though, for industries that use "seating" – busses, trains, airlines – the list is endless. I wonder if McDonald's has any interest in the "seating" industry. Talk about exploiting – one industry feeds the other.

(I don't mean to be insensitive. I'm just super-frustrated.)

February 5, 2007

If there was a theme for today, it would be "lifelines." On the ride in this morning, out of the corner of my eye I glimpsed several sleepy passengers tethered to what my first-glance look appeared to be oxygen lines, or lifelines – a direct connection to some vital resource. I guess it has to do with one's perspective – too many of my older friends and family members lately have been just so tethered to oxygen tanks, both in and out of the hospital. My 80-something-year-old dad, who suffers from chronic obstructive pulmonary disease that developed because of 47 years of smoking, had been connected to an in-home oxygen system with tubes running throughout the house. We joked that, since he'd been hooked up to the contraption, we wouldn't lose him so much; he had a knack for taking off in the electric-powered shopping carts in the local super-sized supermarket after he recovered from a stroke some years earlier. Perhaps it was his only sense of independence as he couldn't drive a car anymore. Actually, he always knew where he was in the supermarket, but my mother frequently lost him.

But, on second glance, these "T" passengers were tethered to IPODs that provided them with a vital supply of who-knows-what! The white ones show up more, the black ones sort of blend in and aren't as noticeable.

I feel that Sue, Mr. Margolis and I are Bob's lifeline and that his supply was cut off some today because of the bitter, near-zero-degree cold. We had all agreed last week that it would be too cold for him to come out today. I even put "Plan B" into effect and took the Green Line one more stop, putting me two blocks closer to my building and the northwest wind at my back. I hope we can reconnect tomorrow.

February 6, 2007

A middle-aged, Betty Boopish-looking woman in a mink coat was escorted onto the subway car in Braintree by a freezing blast of air. I recalled a former friend's comments about her mink coat some years earlier, when it became both unfashionable and unconscionable to own one, that "each one of these minks committed suicide."

Today I got closer to the lady selling papers on the Green Line level at the Park Street "T." I finally could distinguish what she was saying; it used to be that after I climbed the first set of stairs from the Red Line to the Green Line, processed myself through the meat-grinder turnstile, and walked up the next flight of stairs to the plaza above, I would hear her droning on in what I thought was some Portuguese accent, but still not understanding what she said. But, as I had to walk past her to get to the Green Line trolley stop, I finally could make out her words: "Fif-*TEE* cents here, Fif-*TEE* cents here"; she was selling copies of the *Boston Herald*. She was having a solicitation war with "*Metro* guy," who was saying in a somewhat mocking way: "Free, Free!"

In spite of my six layers of turtlenecks, sweaters, a sweatshirt and winter jacket, long underwear and two pairs of pants, two hoods and a face mask, I was still cold walking the two windy blocks to my building from Government Center.

February 7, 2007

The distinctive scent of *Juicy Fruit* gum tagged along after a sulking, sophomoric young man in khaki pants, an oversized jacket, black gloves, sneakers and a cap that was placed so that you couldn't see his eyes. He just fit into the seat next to me. At the next stop there was a musical chairs type of scurry for seats as some people – many students – got off and new folks got on. In the midst of it, the young man next to me got up and headed for a newly vacated seat on the other side of the car. At the same time as he darted for the seat, a blonde woman walked from the bench on the other side of the train intending to sit next to him in his original place. As she did, she looked the boy in the face and demanded, "Sit down!" Without a word, he did, but on the other side of the car. And there he stayed in a rather belabored and angry sulk, never looking up until he got off at the JFK-UMASS stop. I assumed he was going to Boston College High School. I also assumed that the woman was his mother and that she did not want to make a scene on the train. Kids know when and under what circumstances they can get away with that kind of stuff. But I just felt for both of them – it's just such a terrible place when you're in conflict with another person, especially a mother and a son.

It's twelve degrees this morning at 7:30 a.m. in Boston. Regardless, I needed to walk, so I got out at Park Street. I was half hoping to see Bob to give him the food coupons; the other half of my hope was that he wouldn't come out today. The latter won. He said last week on Thursday that he'd be going shopping with the coupons I gave him then, and so I think he had enough food so that he didn't have to come out to the street today. Next time I see Mr. Margolis, we'll need to reopen the conversation about connecting Bob with a social worker to help him get food stamps. Bob mentioned that he was willing to try again, even in spite of the callous treatment he'd experienced years ago.

February 8, 2007

"Oh, Chris, you look so cold," said Bob as he greeted me outside Park Street Church. "I am," I said, "but you look colder." He said that in spite of wearing his parka, he was still cold. He said he was sweating underneath it and then that made him colder – something I remember hearing my cross-country-ski-instructor brother cautioning against once. Bob proudly [thankfully] remarked that he'd been out 12 winters now and still hasn't lost his toes. He said that "Mumbles Menino" [Boston's Mayor Menino] had the police either round up the homeless and put them into shelters for the night or arrest them as a way to get them in from the cold.

He said that he had spent three years, six months and seven days in a federal prison for "doing something stupid as a teenager." He didn't care to elaborate, and I didn't want to pursue it, but he shared that the psychiatrist said it was the result of too little love and too many foster homes. As a contemporary of his, I admitted that we all did some pretty stupid stuff when we were in our teens.

Feeling the cold seeping through all of my layers, and thinking that Bob has been out in this a lot longer than my five minutes talking with him, I asked if I could get him a cup of coffee. He picked up a Styrofoam Dunkin' Donuts cup, saying yes I could as the one he had was cold. I crossed at the light to the shop just across the street and picked up a medium regular coffee for him.

Upon my return, I asked him what he'd been doing these cold winter days. "I just walk the beach; there's nothing much else to do," he said as he shrugged his shoulders. "Looking down at his gloved hand, which held a cigarette that was burning much too near the filter for my comfort, I said, "Don't burn your glove!" He tossed the butt onto the sidewalk. "Sorry," I said, "it looked as if you might ignite any second."

It was time for me to get on to work. He winked and blew me a kiss, saying, "Love ya." I blew one back. "Love ya, too."

February 9, 2007

Waiting for the light before the turn into the Braintree "T" parking garage, an avian chorus screeched through my closed car windows. The source of the cacophony took shelter in the shrubbery.

Taking my seat on the black vinyl bench in the next-to-last car, I noticed a couple of passengers who preferred to stand rather than sit in one of the empty seats. One was a young man in his teens whose baggy jeans were draped with cords of heavy metal chains. Also hooked to an Ipodian lifeline, his head was decorated with multiple rings in his nose, ears and eyebrows. The other passenger was a very tall, very slender young woman who wore black-and-white pinstriped, flared slacks with large cuffs. The cuffs were anchored by large black binder clips – one on each inner seam, one on each outer seam.

Today was, as predicted, one of the coldest days of the winter with the temperature hovering around 0 degrees Fahrenheit. I'm grateful that Bob wasn't out today.

How do the birds keep from freezing in this weather?

February 12, 2007

Looking much older than their years, two twenty-something's boarded the waiting subway car in Braintree. The young man and woman seemed to have been discarded by society. But they had each other, and it was touching to see how each cared for the other. He had an unkempt beard and mustache, an oversize grey parka within which he hid his ungloved hands. The grey hood of a sweatshirt that he was wearing underneath kept his head warm and covered his otherwise sweet boyish face as he slept on the young woman's shoulder. She held a cane – I'm not sure whether it was his or hers – he carried it onto the car and gave it to her as she sat down, but I'm not sure if he actually used it to walk. She was wearing a black parka and jeans with sneakers. She pulled up the turtleneck collar as far as it would go up to her nose, and then she pulled down her hood to cover the rest of her face so she could have some privacy as she slept as well. Perhaps this was their shelter for the day.

February 13, 2007

Riding the train this morning, my thoughts were still focused on last evening's visit to MGH where a dear friend lay unconscious after having suffered a series of strokes. She was encircled by a very loving family who had come to share her last birthday with her...

> *Ginny, what a party last evening! All the kids were there, and they were as gracious and welcoming as always. How we laughed when I told* [her husband] *Bernie that, as a youngster, my son said he hadn't remembered how funny he was. He had really enjoyed his visit a week or so ago with you. He remembered the mashed potatoes you used to make and how that was the only time he had them when he was younger because I didn't make them. I loved the prayer circle and how we all sang to you for your special day.*

As I approached the top of the stairs of the Park Street station, a very large African American lady was fumbling through a shopping bag. She wore a white fuzzy hat, a long white down-looking parka that covered a long white dirndl skirt and white boots and gloves. She was mumbling to herself and then we both walked out onto the plaza together at the same time. She looked over at me and smiled, saying, "Breadcrumbs ... the birds need to eat, too." I smiled and started walking over to meet Bob. Out of the corner of my eye I saw a huge flock of pigeons flying over and landing near her as she flung pieces of bread on the ground. She looked like a big white bird herself.

I had picked up a five-dollar bill on the ground the day before and added it to the extra five dollars that Sue had given me to give to Bob or anyone else who needed it. Bob was there and I offered him our food gift cards with the extra money. Sue had given me a picture album for Bob, but I had forgotten to bring it in. I asked him if he could use it, and he said that he could. Tapping the upper pocket of his jacket he said he kept the disposable camera with him. I would bring the album to him the next time.

It was cold and I felt rushed to get to work, so our conversation was short. He wished me a good day and said, "Good luck with all the fat people!"

February 27, 2007

With a twinkle in his eye, Bob greeted me this morning with, "I have a new job! It's with the Egg Layers Association making a new egg because sales have gone down." He was going to try to make one that would open with Velcro or a zipper. [Droll; very droll!] Then in a more serious tone, he pointed to the tall, unoccupied building across the street, saying that "it hadn't been used in the 12 years that he'd been sitting here." He said that it would make a perfect place to build a shelter for folks like him, giving him easy access to his corner. Last night he'd had a spaghetti dinner at a local place in Revere, near where he lives. The owner knew he was good for the tab later on, as Bob didn't have much to pay him for it. But he was hungry.

"How's Sue?" "She's doing fine." "Send her my best, please."

February 28, 2007

Smells of inky, pulpy newspapers filled the train car this morning. Feeling more tired than usual, I wasn't up for work. Everything felt heavy, including the air now.

When I approached Bob this morning, he was eating three sunny-side-up eggs on a paper plate with a plastic fork – breakfast from John in the church. He also had a banana and a ceramic mug of steaming tea sitting on the sidewalk. I told him not to stop eating as his breakfast would get cold. He wouldn't hear of it and set it down to talk.

He was the one cheering me up today. He asked me how things were going, and I told him I was tired and struggling with my job. "They burned you out?" he asked. "I feel that way," I said.

He says that lots of folks he sees are looking for work and "businesses want just young, bubbly people." I agreed, acknowledging that I was old but used to be "bubbly." I had remembered job hunting over the last few years. While I was "deflated" for the time being, I was still grateful to be employed. And tomorrow's another day.

Wanting to be encouraging to him, I asked how his writing was going. He hadn't looked at it in a long time. Maybe when the weather's better he can sit outside at the beach and do some.

Time to get to work. "Hope you can cure all the fat people," he called after me as I started on my way.

March 1, 2007

A medical emergency at Broadway Station left our train suspended between JFK/UMASS and Andrew Station for 20 minutes. I looked out the window at the awakening suburbs to the west, and I saw newly erected scaffolding surrounding a distant church steeple. I thought that, under other circumstances, Bob might be up there or in a place very much like it. It must take a strong constitution to do that kind of work in this sub-freezing weather.

March 7, 2007

It's a full six degrees in Boston and I bet that Bob wouldn't come out today, so I hopped on the Green Line to Government Center for the shorter, two-block walk to work. Walking across the plaza, I passed the same fellow that I saw yesterday, emptying trash barrels. I thought of my friend's prayer last evening for protection for all the folks who have to work out in this bitter cold. I saw he had a public works truck running nearby parked on the plaza, so I trusted that he would be able to escape there to warm up from time to time. I thought about my son and hoped he'd worn a warm coat and hat on his way to work. I guess mothers still want to protect their children no matter how old they are.

Tomorrow is Thursday, and it's supposed to be just a little bit warmer – maybe in the teens. But there also may be some snow. I hope I'll be able to give Bob the food coupons then.

March 13, 2007

"Chris, Sweetheart, I missed you!" exclaimed Bob as I approached. Last week was the coldest in the entire winter with double-digit, sub-zero wind chills. My assumption was that Bob wouldn't be out in that kind of weather. But, to my chagrin and disbelief, he told me that he had been out on his corner on Friday in the 4 degrees; he was hungry and he stayed out until 11:30 that morning. I hadn't come into the city on Friday, but that was the only day he was there.

Bob shared that he had gotten a letter from his landlord. He said that all the people living in his building got a letter saying it was going to be bulldozed soon and that they would have to look for another place to live. Bob was really depressed about it. He didn't think he could move – physically or mentally. The thought of it sent him into another depression. So, I said optimistically (wanting to make lemonade out of this lemon he'd been thrown), this may be an opportunity then for us to follow-up with Mr. Margolis and look into reopening his application with the Coalition to End Senior Homelessness. He said that Mr. Margolis had talked with him about that just yesterday and was indeed going to look into it. So I told him I'd do whatever I could to support him with that. And as far as moving, I'm sure that, between Mr. Margolis and me, we could scare up a crew of folks to help him physically move his stuff to wherever the next place would be.

Then he told me that a few days ago he had gone to a Chinese food place and had gotten a cup of wonton soup and, with it, a fortune cookie. He pulled out the fortune cookie insert that he had saved, and shared it with me: "You will move into a beautiful new home within the next year." So, there is a task ahead!

I told him I hadn't seen Mr. Margolis now for three weeks or so but to let him know that I'd be willing to help with whatever needed doing. He said that Mr. Margolis had talked about going to Paris soon, and that he did that usually once a year. He went with his wife, who, Bob said, was a really smart lady and did historical research of some sort. He said they were great people – just like "matched bookends." We agreed that it's great when you can find your "bookend."

As I was getting ready to leave, a familiar fellow (to Bob) walked by looking for a light for his cigarette. He was a slight man with long-ish, messy brown hair and what looked like birthmarks on his face. He was wearing a black patch over his left eye and had an unlit stump of a cigarette clutched between his teeth. Bob remarked, "What happened to you!?" He had been beaten up again. Bob handed him his lighter. The man tried to light the cigarette with his right hand only. He was disabled and kept his left arm in his jacket pocket. He nearly set his hair and jacket on fire as the wind fanned the flame. Bob pulled out a pack of matches instead and switched them for the lighter. He said, "Here take these – you can keep 'em." The man tried lighting the butt with a match, but the wind blew it out. Bob instructed him to go around the corner of the church where it was somewhat protected from the wind. He did, and Bob and I talked a bit more. Then the man came back, unsuccessful again, and said, "Do you have a good cigarette?" Bob replied that he didn't know if there was any such thing, but he handed him a fresh one from his pack. He took it and went back around the corner to light it. As Bob and I were finishing up our conversation, the man came around the corner to say thanks and we wished him a good day. Bob said he'd been "out here" as long as he had been – 12 years, and it's amazing that he's lasted this long. The man couldn't understand how Bob could have managed on his corner either, but Bob said he'd made some good friends along the way.

I told him that I had to get off to work, gave him the food cards and said that I'd probably only see him on Wednesday. Friday was "Evacuation Day" for Boston employees and I was going to evacuate. He said, "Just don't run away from me!" I said that I wouldn't, wished him a good day and was on my way.

March 14, 2007

The flat-roofed triple-deckers bordering the tracks in Dorchester always seem to be leaning as we go by. But, a closer look shows that their roofs are constructed with an intentional, ever-so-slight slant to allow rain and snow to drain or slide off. They reminded me of earlier times when, as a child, my sister and I stayed with my Swedish grandparents for a week during summer vacation in their triple-decker on Louise Street in Worcester. We used to "play house" in the middle of the kitchen floor with my grandmother's matched set of enamel saucepans and utensils. There, she would indulge us with *Kellogg's Sugar Pops* in little green plastic bowls that were made in the shape of row boats. My grandfather, who was home on strike from the steel company, would sit at the table with us, smoking a cigarette, wearing his white T-shirt and work pants. I don't remember that he said much. But I remember, once when he came to visit my family in Bristol, New Hampshire, at my maternal grandfather's farmhouse where we also vacationed as kids, while holding my [then] toddler brother and sitting in one of the dark-green Kennedy rocking chairs on the porch, he would rock and stop quickly, making my little brother scream with laughter.

March 19, 2007

Seven a.m. and a new week begins. For me, it's aboard a Red Line train making the now-routine trip from the Braintree "T" to Boston. For one of my sisters, who has been spending time living on the coast of Southern Maine for the winter, the day starts at Logan Airport in a plane that's taking off at the same time for Los Angeles, with the final destination being Santa Barbara, her west-coast home, for a few weeks. Such different lives.

Two young high school students hopped on the train soon after we went underground. One was wearing an oversized dark brown winter jacket, a dark blue ski cap, sneakers and khaki chinos, the waist of which was hanging just around the bottom of the jacket. The crotch of the slacks was at the level of his knees, and I was sure one would see his backside if he leaned over. How in the world did they stay up?! If he had to run, he'd never make it!

In my usual seat next to one of the doors of the train, at South Station I heard a banjo being tuned. So I turned and looked over my right shoulder and there was an older, grey-haired fellow in a black beret, a brown jacket and black slacks sitting on a bench there plucking the strings and turning the pegs to get them in tune. The banjo was connected to a small electric amplifier. Also connected to the amplifier by a black leather leash was a handsome black German Shepherd reclining on the concrete floor. I had my camera handy in my bag and was so tempted to whip it out and take his picture before the door closed, but that felt like stealing something very valuable.

Monday is Bob's "day off" and I didn't really expect him to be at his spot. But, I'll have double the food coupons from last week and this for him later in the week when I see him. A huge flock of pigeons greeted the "bird lady" – maybe she was actually an angel, too – as she walked onto the plaza at Park Street. "They have to eat, too," I remember her telling me some weeks ago. There was a headline about new transitional housing arrangements for homeless veterans that I saw on the news today. I wonder if Bob would reconsider … I'm going to research it.

March 22, 2007

The continuing competition between *Metro* guy and, "fifty cents here, fifty cents here" greeted me again as I emerged from the bowels of Park Street Station. They followed me as I went through the "meat grinder" and up the next flight of stairs to the street above. As I approached the exit, I anxiously looked through the glass window to see if Bob was there. Thank heaven he was! I had two weeks' worth of "apples and pears" to give him (the food vouchers have pictures of apples and pears).

Bob greeted me with a big smile as he pointed to the top of the building across the street – it was the red-tailed hawk again. "He's huge!" I remarked as I looked up at the hawk. In spite of his smile, Bob's right foot was giving him trouble today. "You can't see anything. When I showed the doctor, I said, 'you can't see anything.' The pain is inside." Did Tylenol help it? He said he took lots of aspirins each day and it doesn't seem to help.

Offering some sympathy, I then changed the subject: "What's new on the housing front?" I asked him. "I've got until November," he said. So there was somewhat of a "stay" of execution. I suggested that when Mr. Margolis gets back from his trip, maybe we could talk about options if that's what he would like us to do. Then I asked him about a social worker, and did he find one. He said that he didn't, and I asked him if he would like me to see if I could look into that for him. I told him that I felt everyone needs an advocate, and he surely should be entitled to one. He said that in all this time he'd been out here, he never had one, and that, yes, he would like me to do that.

He asked how I was doing and I said that things had been going better, but that I had had a call from my dad early yesterday morning saying that he had fallen again in the bathroom and my mother had to call 9-1-1 to have the EMTs help get him up again. He had suffered a stroke some years ago. I told Bob that I asked my dad if he needed me to come up and help with anything and Bob said that it's right for people to help "their fellow man." He said the first line in that order should be your parents. He said he never knew his mother, but he stayed by his father's side the last four months of his life while his dad was in the hospital dying of cancer. He had worked with his dad in the roofing business and one day his dad asked Bob for an aspirin. Bob said he never took anything. Next day he was in the hospital suffering with cancer throughout his body. He was dead within four months. Bob had stopped work to be with him. He said "Ma Bell" was bugging him about his phone bill after a while. Bob explained that he'd not been working so that he could be with his father, and the Operator asked if she could speak with the hospital. She did and then called Bob and said not to worry about the bill at all. We both wished "Ma Bell" was back.

He asked, "How's Sue?" I assured him she was well, and that she had had a clean bill of health in terms of the glaucoma and just had to deal with having two cataracts removed. He was relieved in hearing that news.

It was then time to get to work. We wished each other well ... spring was "threatening" and we were looking forward to a milder day today. "See you tomorrow ... have a good day," I said. Nodding his head, he said, "Weather permitting."

March 26, 2007

The ride to Boston started out under a cotton-candy ribbon cloud that stretched half-way around the sky like a rainbow, but just made of bright pink fluff. The train was full at the start, which most likely meant there had been delays somewhere along the line. While driving over the Neponset River Bridge between the North Quincy and JFK/UMASS stations, a young man collapsed. Somehow, everyone made room for him and propped him on the seat; he was breathing and had a pulse but he was unresponsive. "Hit the alarm button!" "Call 9-1-1" "He has a pulse!" were called out in succession by various riders. One Good Samaritan made his way from the other end of the car to the young man who was drooped on the bench. The rescuer had a cell phone and phoned ahead asking for an ambulance to meet the train at JFK Station. He stayed with him and tried to get him to speak. The patient was woozy when we arrived at JFK and the Good Samaritan helped him out to the bench on the station platform and stayed there until help came.

Wow, what selflessness.

Bob was in his spot today and said he had a new job. It seemed that the IFAW (the International Federation of Animal Welfare) was trying to decide if zebras were actually black with white stripes or white with black stripes and he was going to try to do something about that. I suggested that he'd have more trouble than he knew what to do with if he changed their stripes from vertical to horizontal. That would only create a lot of vain and self-conscious lady zebras. Well, then, maybe he would work with leopards, connecting their spots to make patterns or pictures.

Just then, around the corner came an older man, short only in stature, tall in accomplishments. "Hello, Professor!" exclaimed Bob as he recognized him. He was perhaps in his 70's, about five feet, six inches tall, and very nicely dressed. He had a long grey beard and wore a hat. He was holding onto something that looked like a combination cane and scooter which had a small British flag emblem on it. There was a cane handle onto which he held, and attached to it were a couple of brief cases.

Bob introduced me to him, though I forget his name. He was a professor from Suffolk University, and I imagine he was the one who arranged for Bob to speak in some of his classes. The professor told me that Bob was quite an artist, he did etchings on slate. He told Bob that he would get him some more slates if he needed them. I agreed with the professor that Bob was indeed an artist and that I had seen his work. Bob offered that he was still working on one for me. I remarked at how "cool" the professor's cane/scooter was. He said they sold them in England but they didn't make them anymore. Just as he said that, two young children rode by on scooters. [Cute, God, very cute!]

He asked me what an "Obesity Society" did [my bag that I carry has that printed on the outside], and I explained that it was a research group and I had gotten the bag from a conference I attended. They both said that I wasn't a good candidate if I were promoting obesity. [I guess that was a compliment!]

As I was late from the long, eventful train ride, I wished them both a good day. I also thought I'd let the two of them catch up.

March 27, 2007

Today I boarded another ill-fated train. Somewhere around the Quincy Adams stop, I started smelling smoke, but wasn't sure of its source. As we continued on, at each stop it seemed more and more pronounced. I didn't say anything to anyone, but wondered if anyone else noticed. No one seemed to give it any thought as they had their noses in their *Metros* or were snoozing. Why didn't I say something? At JFK Station, a smoky smell was quite present in the car. The doors closed, the train started forward for a split second and then stopped. The doors opened and the words, "This train is disabled. No passengers please. This train is disabled. No passengers, please," were announced over the loudspeaker. Grumbling ensued as the passengers "de-trained."

Another announcement said that the next inbound train was approaching on another platform, so everyone scurried and scrambled [in an every-man-for-himself kind of way] upstairs, over and downstairs to the other platform to be first in line. While there were no seats available, we all crammed in, and the train was on its way.

While it was a milder day today, it had rained earlier this morning, and Bob didn't come to Park Street today.

April 4, 2007

Today I'm somewhat sleepy – not as sharp as I'd like to be. Except that I've noticed the "routine" of things. Seeing some of the same folks come and go (along with me) each day, the familiar sounds and sights, like "sports guy" with all the jewelry and a Boston Red Sox cap, the high school kids at the top of the stairs just inside the Park Street Station entrance every Wednesday. Even the drive to Braintree is now uneventful, taking a predictable 30 minutes each day. I was glad to see the young man and his mother on the train, whom I had seen some weeks ago when they obviously had had a bad morning. They were in a much friendlier place together today. That, too, is the cycle of things. Forgiveness and reconciliation are wonderful things!

Bob stayed in today.

April 9, 2007

I had a restless night. There's no rhyme or reason to it, but sometimes I just can't get to sleep for a couple of hours and then, when I do, I wake up again in an hour or so. It takes over an hour to get back to sleep. This morning I had awakened around 2:30 a.m. and must have drifted back to sleep around 4 or so, which is dangerous because then it's much harder getting up at 4:30 a.m. I must have hit the snooze button a number of times because, when I finally realized that I should get up, it was around 5:15 a.m. This meant the day would be out of balance. My early morning routine of coffee, reading and then playing my guitar would have to be abbreviated today if I were to make it to the Braintree T early enough to get a parking space.

A strong smell of disinfectant at the T station gagged me as I walked up the stairs to the platform. I took an end seat as usual and, as the 7 a.m. commuter train pulled in to the station on the adjacent track, an anorexic-looking girl with a hard-shell trombone case entered the car and sat across from me. I must have dozed most of the way in as I was at Park Street in no time.

Bob was there today after several days' absence. He said he had had the flu. He also said that the cops had been kicking folks off the sidewalk outside the *7-11* and *Dunkin' Donuts* across the street for arguing and jingling paper cups at passers by. To be fair, they had to include Bob, too. He was "laying low" for a few days.

He told me about the time he had suicidal thoughts – he said he had a "downtown down" once when he was sitting in a bar at Revere Beach. He'd been drinking too much and said he just wanted to end it all. So he picked himself up and started walking into the ocean. He was just going to walk and walk until it was over – even though he was a good swimmer. But, as fate (or luck!?) would have it, apparently he was walking on a sandbar. He just kept walking and walking, but the water didn't get higher. After a time, he said he wasn't drunk anymore and he turned around and went back to the bar to finish his beer.

April 24, 2007

Magnolia-petal "snow" was falling on the Granary Burial Ground this morning and spilling over onto the Tremont Street sidewalk. There was a sweet fragrance in the air, but I didn't know if it was coming from the flowers on the tree or not. Spring was indeed in the air this mild morning. While Bob wasn't anywhere to be seen, the other regulars were everywhere – the folk who passed by the corner of Tremont and Park Streets on their way to work or school or whatever their destination. The Suffolk University professor was [jay] walking across Tremont Street when there was a lull in the traffic. Mr. Jones, from the Thursday morning group, and the others crossed from the Park Street Station to walk up toward the State House. This would be a great day for Bob to be out, but he had told me recently that the police were "cleaning up the place" again, so he was being somewhat cautious about being there. Maybe tomorrow...

April 26, 2007

Thursday again and Bob was there. While he had a cup of *Dunkin' Donuts* coffee sitting on the ground next to him, a coffee-in-a-keg-clad squadron of young people stopped by and offered us both a free cup of coffee in which we might try a sample of *Coffee-Mate*. I declined, but Bob accepted. They fumbled around filling the cup with the "do-hickie" attached to the cord coming from the keg, but then they withdrew their offer because the coffee was cold. No matter ... up the street they went to their supply van and replaced the cold keg for one with hot coffee in it. They came back and poured a hot sample into a small Styrofoam cup in which they also poured the non-dairy creamer. Bob's *Dunkin' Donuts* coffee had toppled over somehow and was streaming down the sidewalk

Mr. Jones then walked over to speak with us. It was getting late, so I left for work and let the two of them finish talking together.

May 2, 2007

I planned a few days' rest after finishing some major projects at work – to get balanced. I drove to Maine to have lunch and a short visit with my parents and my sister. During the visit I was urged once again by my mother to try wearing makeup – a life-long pursuit of hers. To me the very word "makeup" suggests "make believe" and saying that I ought to adopt this practice is tantamount to saying "you can't be who you really are [because you're not acceptable to society that way] so you'll have to put on a facade and just pretend to be this or that." But my final thought on the subject [because I don't want to spend anymore time thinking about this] is: makeup is anti-truth.

May 9, 2007

All I heard this morning while riding the "T" was the synchronistic rattle-ruffle turning of newspaper pages. How this noise was heard over the rattle-clack-clack of the subway car along the tracks is hard to understand. Maybe it's just a matter of tuning out something that's become familiar and repetitive and realigning one's focus. I'm sleepy this morning and not focusing on much else.

I was energized by the refreshing 66-degree spring air that greeted me as I emerged from Park Street. Bob was sitting across the street talking with one of his "regulars." I walked over and stood in line to greet him. As the former left and I moved up to first place in line, he excused himself for lighting up a cigarette, but he hadn't had one for days. He asked me how things were going; I told him that I had decided to turn down a job offer I had received a few weeks earlier. I shared my thoughts about a reading this morning [from *The Language of Letting Go*] about how it seemed that situations repeat themselves because there's a lesson you have to learn from the situation, and that it, or something similar to it, will keep presenting itself until you learn whatever it is you're supposed to learn from it.

I asked him if he knew about the "Common Cathedral" that was held on Sunday afternoons on Boston Common. He had heard about them and I said that we [the musical trio that I'm in] were thinking about playing for it, and that maybe we'd see him there sometime. He said, "Maybe."

May 11, 2007

As I sat on the train this morning awaiting the start of our trek into town, I saw a "90-degree lady" – bent over from the waist in a right angle – emerge from the staircase, walk past the window and enter the next car. I don't know if it was a severe case of osteoporosis or other physical deformity.

Recognizing my own proclivity for developing it, and not wanting to make fun of the afflicted, but, rather, wanting to inform and educate, I wrote *My Back Ages* (with apologies to Bob Dylan):

> *Calcium and exercise have now become routine,*
> *and Starbucks should be off my list – the culprit is caffeine.*
> *In my youth these healthful words were overlooked somehow.*
> *Ah, 'cause I was so much taller then, I'm shorter than that now.*

Bob's mood was low again today. It's just plain tough existing and scraping together enough to cover his room and day-to-day living expenses. I was humbled when he told me about a lady he had seen in the supermarket an evening or so before. [Sue and] I had given him $60 in food gift cards earlier that week, one for $50 and one for $10. He was shopping, driving himself around the store in one of the motorized shopping carts. He said he noticed another shopper, a woman who was destitute, "lifting" stuff. Bob drove up to her and gave her the $10 gift card and wished her well. Talk about grace.

May 15, 2007

Three commuters on the bench across from me provided this morning's entertainment. One was a middle-aged man, dressed in business casual, minding his own business and reading the *Metro*. A space away from him sat a very slender, 40-ish-looking woman with shoulder-length brown hair. She was casually dressed in a white-striped pink over-blouse and light pink slacks to match. She had a large bag that she placed on the floor in front of her. In the seat between the two of them – the only one left on the train – sat a very broad-shouldered middle-eastern-looking gentleman with an angular build. [To the frustration of the first gentleman on his right] wedging himself in, he placed his broad shoulders flat against the back of the seat and opened his full-sized *Boston Globe*. Displaced by this maneuver, the first man's left shoulder was now forced up higher than his right. He was pinned in and didn't have any space to wiggle free. He sat that way most of the trip. His eyes alternately shot scowls and then "daggers" at the man in the middle every 30 seconds or so. But the latter man didn't notice as he was distracted from reading his newspaper by the woman to his left who was laboriously applying her makeup. Very carefully and deliberately she outlined her lips with one color, painted on a slightly lighter color that matched her fingernails with a lip brush to the rest of her mouth, then a final gloss. With each application, she'd take the time to fish around in the large bag on the floor in front of her for the appropriate item.

Anti-truth.

Bob was very anxious and shaking this morning when I saw him. Mr. Margolis arrived just as he was telling me that he had been approached by a police officer and told to "cease and desist" hanging out on "his corner." Bob pulled out a citation that the officer had given him. He had given Bob a ticket for "aggravated solicitation"! Now I've heard everything, I told him. Bob said it was because the officer couldn't ignore him while he had to scold the folks across the street that were shaking coins in paper cups at, and asking people for money as they walked by. Bob repeated the story of how he asked only once for spare change and about how he would never do it again because of the verbal bashing he received. He was afraid of getting arrested and not being able to sit there and see all of the people who had befriended him over the years – it was his life.

Bob asked Mr. Margolis, "Can you do something with this?" Indeed he could. He would write a letter on Bob's behalf. He assured him that he hadn't done anything wrong, recounting that he understood that Bob had asked for and received permission from the church management to be there. We remembered that they even make breakfast sometimes and bring it out to him. One also has a right to sit on the sidewalk he said. We both tried to allay his fears for the time being.

As Mr. Margolis and I walked on to work, we talked about the status of an application for housing for homeless seniors that he had been working on. I told him I would see about what other options there might be for Bob concerning treatment for his diabetes and he suggested contacting Joslin Clinic. I told him I had learned about some day programs in the city where Bob could go and be with other people. I would try to get more details on them. We exchanged cards and rededicated our efforts to help him.

May 16, 2007

The *ITA Software Company* has given us "T" passengers another challenge: "If the integers from 1 to 999,999,999 were written as words and concatenated, what would the 51 billionth letter be?" Maybe my sister, Phyllis, or my brother, David, knows.

May 21, 2007

A different "commute" today: an all-expenses-paid [by work] trip to Atlanta to a conference at the CDC, the Center for Disease Control and Prevention. They don't include the "P" in the acronym, I guess, because people wouldn't know what CDCP was, as they've called it the CDC for so long. Anyway, I'll return home on Thursday.

As I get older I've been feeling more and more like I'm straddling two worlds: one foot is in June Cleaver's and, the other, in Gloria Steinham's. Growing up in a middle-of-the-middle-class culture, I wasn't expecting, nor was I expected to work in the world of business and go jet-setting to conferences and the like. No, I expected/was expected to go to college and graduate with a diamond ring and the hope of living happily ever after, volunteering in my community and making a home for my husband and children and probably a dog. It's just like in the song, "Me and My Gal," that my dad used to sing to me when I was a little girl [an odd choice for a song, now that I think of it]: "...We're gonna build a little home for two or three or four or more in love land, for me and my gal!" I would find love and security and fulfillment as a homemaker; I would be taken care of. If I worked at all it would be "mother's hours" at a school or as a nurse or in retail somewhere.

In the 50's and 60's when I was growing up, secretaries working regular business hours were usually not married and generally quit working after they were to become homemakers. That's what I expected I'd do after working as a secretary myself. But that is not my reality.

May 24, 2007

The CDC in Atlanta was a fortress – several futuristically designed buildings in a massive compound surrounded by a wall and a gate. The building in which we were meeting even had something like a moat around one side. You couldn't get into the building without passing an armed guard and you had to place your things on the conveyor belt to be X-rayed as you walked through the metal detector, just like at the airport. The conference was OK; I learned some new things and made some new contacts.

On my return trip home, walking toward the "Atrium" to get to the security check point at the Atlanta Airport, I heard the sound of soft applause. It grew louder and louder as I approached and, as I drew nearer, a hundred or so US Army soldiers in their fatigues and loaded backpacks marched double file along the perimeter of the sun-lit space through to the security check. Of all folks?! Why did they need to be checked?! I thought of clapping – not because I supported the war by any spin of the imagination, but just to show support. As the applause grew louder and louder still, and as people started standing up as the soldiers marched by, I couldn't clap. I cried instead. I just stood there in the middle of the Atrium and cried. They were all so young. I thought of my 25-year-old son and how, several years ago when he was in college, he and his fellow classmates all had wanted to enlist in the service after the events of 9/11. CNN yesterday and the day before was full of the news of the potential discovery of the body of one of the three soldiers kidnapped in Iraq. I just cried.

Spring-green ivy graffiti decorated the concrete wall alongside Route 3 South near South Boston By-Pass Road. On this, the next-to-last leg of my "commute" home, the "common carrier" in which I rode with a lighted "BRAINTREE" sign on the front, was the Logan Express bus. It will be good to get home.

June 5, 2007

A middle-aged man, [business] casually dressed and wearing oxblood penny loafers (without the pennies) sat across from me on the train this morning. I have some loafers just like his hibernating somewhere in my closet at home. On the floor in front of him sat a brown leather briefcase. I used to carry one of those, too, in my earlier work days. These things felt familiar. They are from another time.

Bob was standing and talking to Mr. Margolis this morning when I approached him on the corner. He had been somewhat displaced by the beginnings of a re-roofing project at the Park Street Church. Blue scaffolding was being erected there on the sidewalk, but it hadn't reached his spot yet. A former roofer himself, Bob couldn't understand why they were replacing a slate roof.

Joining them in their conversation, I listened as Mr. Margolis suggested to Bob that the doctor that he saw at the Monday morning "clinic for the homeless" at MGH could help him with the housing application that he had been working on for him. We also spoke about the application for him for free care at the Joslin Diabetes Center that I had arranged to be mailed to me, and had received at home; I felt badly that I had left it there in my rush to get out this morning. But I would bring it the next day.

While we were talking, a young man stopped by with three packages of cookies and some spare change. He gave them to Bob and said, "God bless!" Bob thanked him graciously and placed them in his open cigar box on the sidewalk.

I told Bob I would bring the application form on Wednesday and would he be here tomorrow? He said he would since it was going to be another nice spring day. Mr. Margolis offered that he wouldn't be there tomorrow as he was putting his boat in the water for the season. I was pleased to learn a little bit about wooden boats, too, as he and Bob went on to relate boat minutiae.

Then it was time to get to work.

June 6, 2007

I woke up this morning with a tune that seemed to want to connect itself to the words: "Why must the ravages of war redeem the freedom of a people?" I hummed it with some of the words into my cassette tape player so that I wouldn't forget the tune; but it appears that wouldn't be necessary. I couldn't stop singing it to myself the whole commute ... the same phrase over and over like a meditation. I thought of the comment that I had heard: "If the answer is 'war,' then we're asking the wrong question." I remembered a segment on NPR sometime last year about the government wanting to create a Department of Peace, but that it received so much flack from politicians – "We'd all look like sissies" – that it never took off. I wondered if it was a spoof or something. Do people actually think like that? We have a lot more evolving to do... *Turn the other cheek.*

Anyway, the war theme played out on the "T" also this morning. Somewhere along the route, the train picked up some teenagers commuting to school; they were loud and disrespectful to each other, not to mention to the other passengers on the train. They used hurtful and filthy words. When they got off they continued "warring" with words at each other. I was sad for them. If peace could only start at home ... what was home like for them...

As I walked out onto the plaza at Park Street, I noticed the blue metal scaffolding had imprisoned more of Park Street Church. As I walked further down Tremont Street, there was more being erected around the Parker House. At the corner of Tremont and School Streets, the traffic light was oddly pointing in the wrong direction – it was backwards, and if it had been the only one on the corner, it could have caused not a little commotion.

Today there is chaos.

June 7, 2007

A short, middle-aged woman sat in the seat across from me this morning on the "T." She had in her lap two *Metro* newspapers and was juggling a large tote bag with a large plastic bag from the *Christmas Tree Shop*. At first I wondered if she had picked up a second newspaper for a friend or colleague, but the next instant she took one of them and laid it open on the floor space just in front of her. Then, setting her feet squarely on the two sides of the paper, she put her tote bag on it, upon which she then placed her shopping bag. As the train started out for Boston, she opened her other *Metro* to read the news of the day.

After we picked up passengers at the Quincy Adams station, the torture began. I couldn't actually tell where it came from, but, seemingly over the loudspeaker, came this high-pitched sound – something like a screaming tea kettle, but more needling, like a smoke detector. At first I thought someone was fiddling with their hearing aid and how they make that piercing sound that drills into your skull through your ears. But it was significantly more ubiquitous. I tried to half cover my ears for the duration, but felt a bit conspicuous in doing so. (It didn't stop until we reached South Station.)

While I had been awake since 3 a.m., I couldn't have dozed if I wanted to, which I did. For some reason I got stuck thinking about a title for my song about calcium and exercise and preventing osteoporosis, which I was practicing for a gig coming up on Sunday. It's to the tune to *My Back Pages* by Bob Dylan and I was trying to think of something clever: "My Back Shrinketh" ... "My

Back Hunch-eth"… I couldn't think of anything that would work. After a trip to the bathroom and back to bed, it hit me. I was only one letter away from being clever – I took the "P" out of the original title and ended up with "My Back Ages." Sometimes it helps not to try so hard and just listen.

I was also thinking about, anticipating being criticized about not participating in a role play at work a few days ago. We were learning the dos and don'ts about testifying at a town meeting on the subject of promoting nutrition and physical activity in schools and so forth (as there are a lot of bills being generated this year on the topic). I usually like to choose when, where and in front of whom I will look ridiculous. If I were actually going to go to a town meeting, I would be very prepared. Speaking "off-the-cuff" is not one of my strong points. I know this about myself. It's like bungee jumping – it's something that I never [willingly] need to do. (I wonder where the phrase "off-the-cuff" came from. Does it mean you write notes on the cuff of your shirt and …)

Anyway, if I did prepare, I would make it entertaining as well as educational. Unaccompanied, I would sing *My Back Ages*, after which I would further introduce myself as an aging "Boomer" who had been diagnosed recently with "early thinning of the bones." I would explain that if we ate nutritious foods and were more physically active in all parts of our lives, this debilitating condition might be prevented. Then I would quiz them to see if they could remember at least one of three things from the song that would help them remember how to prevent it.

All of this is to say that I missed an opportunity … I hope I don't miss the next one. I hope there *is* one. Well, on with the day.

June 13, 2007

Bob was standing on the sidewalk just outside the maturing scaffolding at the church, finishing a conversation with Margolis … something about living in a commercial bread truck …maybe I didn't hear that correctly, but you never know.

Not knowing where to start, I just jumped in and asked Bob if the sand castle contest would be held again on Revere Beach on Labor Day weekend. He assured me that, yes, every year they were there, but he said "the Feds own the beach now and that they cut the lifeguard stands in half." Mr. Margolis commented that this must "make it hard for the lifeguards to stand" which resulted in a smirk from Bob and a laugh from me. Anyway, Mr. Margolis brought up the subject of Bob's housing application, which helped me remember to produce from my tote bag the Joslin Clinic free care application form that I had remembered today. I hope this will help him get the care he needs and give him some comfort, if not peace of mind.

June 19, 2007

Having my sister as a companion on the way to work this morning made me think about how much of my life has become habit and routine – not mundane, but there are certain timings and expectations that just become automated over time. It's not good or bad; it just *is*.

After reaching Park Street, because of a small problem with her knee, we sought out the escalator instead of the stairs. We found it. But, thinking a woman's caution – "It's not working" – meant that the meat-grinder turnstile wasn't working (or so it seemed because someone tried to push it and it looked like it was just stuck), I pushed my way through the other one to find that it was the escalator that wasn't working. Through the bars I tried to explain to my sister on the other side how to navigate to the usual set of stairs up one flight and then to the escalator that would take her up the second flight. But, she decided to come with me as I think my directions were mostly just confusing and there was no possibility of me returning through the meat-grinder. So we walked up two levels on the malingering escalator. We passed an elderly Asian woman who was having trouble with the stairs; she got stuck there, too. I realized this about two-thirds of the way up and called down to her to see if she needed help. With a grand smile she said, "Thank you," and that she was all right.

We reached the top on Tremont Street, right across from Bob's corner at the Park Street Church. He wasn't there today.

June 21, 2007

On the train this morning, a pair of elementary-school-aged Asian eyes sparkled between two "standees"– one, his mother and, the other, the lady who had given the young boy her seat. He was all innocence.

Mr. Margolis was talking with Bob about a gentleman from Brookline that he knew who had passed by to attend the Thursday morning prayer breakfast just up the street. He was going to stop by to see Bob afterward to discuss looking into housing for him in Brookline. I asked Mr. Margolis whether it was a town or a city; indeed, it's still a town. Anyway, Bob was looking forward to that possibility.

Bob changed the subject and said he was bothered by the pain [etiology unknown] in his feet again; it was also in his right hand today. I asked him if he needed any help in filling out the form for Joslin. He clicked his fingers and said, "Nuts, I forgot to bring it." I asked if he'd have any trouble getting some kind of statement or rent receipt from his landlord to accompany the form. "Why did they need that," asked Mr. Margolis. "They need to document his financial status to consider him for free care," I said. "He has to document that he is destitute." Bob said he didn't think he could except for the scraps of paper that he received in exchange for the cash for the rent of his room; he saved them every month. Receipts nonetheless, we both offered to photocopy them all so he could submit this proof with the application. He didn't want to let them go, but we explained that we'd just photocopy them for him to send with the application, and that he'd get the originals back to hold on to. Mr. Margolis assured Bob that he wouldn't be the first person in the world to do this. Bob seemed to be OK with that, and I think he will entrust the errand to Mr. Margolis.

Lawrence, the man at the security desk where I work died suddenly of a heart attack on Tuesday. There were flowers and a memorial book to sign in the lobby this morning when I came in. I've known him for only a little over a year now. He greeted me and everyone else who worked there by name, every single day. I thought he worked for the Department, but learned that he just worked for the security company that was under contract for the building. He had no health insurance. We're all contributing to a fund for his family to help with burial expenses. He was an angel among angels. His living inspired me to be gracious; his passing reminded me that we only have today.

June 22, 2007

It's Friday, and, to my surprise, Bob was there today. He was sitting under the scaffolding that now pretty much enveloped the church. But he got up and walked out from under it to chat. As we shook hands, he said he was "recovering from yesterday – bad insulin," (which, he said, affected his arm, but was better today) and apparently "bad blood" in the form of his landlord who had done his best to, and apparently succeeded in intimidating Bob for underpayment of his rent at the bar yesterday. I think that's why Bob was out today.

At any rate he said he had connected with the man from Brookline yesterday and had made an appointment to meet him on Monday. They would go together to the housing authority to see what might be done for him. I'm so pleased that Mr. Margolis has been able to leverage yet another possibility for housing through yet another advocate!

June 28, 2007

My "automatic pilot" was suspended briefly this morning as my sister awakened early and came downstairs to make coffee and chat. I was gyrating between the kitchen and bathroom, brushing my teeth, packing my lunch, making coffee-to-go, and putting the trash together, and I was stopped [gladly] in mid-circuit as she told me of the news of her daughter's exceptional success during her first year of college – she got a "1" in politics at Cambridge University, and, I'm told they don't give out many of those. Hoorays are in order!

Bob and Mr. Margolis were standing talking just under the scaffolding at the church. "Good Mornings!" all around. I produced a manila envelope with the copies and originals of Bob's rent receipts and gave them to him. He was grateful and said he'd attach the copy to the application form. So here's hoping.

He said that he would see Mr. Jones after the Thursday morning prayer breakfast today and they would go to Brookline to check out housing options. I remarked that he had options now, but Bob didn't want to get his hopes up. But, he said, "That's the trouble, I always get my hopes up." I reminded him that he was human and that's what humans do. He jokingly agreed and said that was the trouble – that he's human!

I asked him again about his writing and said he hadn't gotten to it yet, but that there was this "little voice" that he heard every time he looked at the stack of papers. He said, "I hear your voice saying, 'How's you're writing coming along?'" He said that sometimes he thinks that he can only write when under pressure. I agreed, as that's been my experience many times, too. He said that maybe a lightning bolt would hit him and provide the necessary impetus to do it. I told him that he should probably look forward to that coming this afternoon, as the forecast said there would be lots of lightning later today. Jonathan was prepared as he was holding an umbrella.

It was time to go and I told him, "Sue said to say 'Hi!'"

"Hi to Sue, and tell her thanks, too."

Friday, June 29, 2007

I sat on the opposite side of the train this morning, facing east. The sky was overcast anyway, so no problem with the sun in my eyes, and I wanted to get a seat on the Boston-bound train [whose departure was imminent, said the bell] rather than leisurely wait for the next one. As the train's brakes hissed, I prepared myself for the lurch of the train that would make me teeter to the left. But, the joke was on me as my body "slapstick-ishly" pitched to the right – I forgot I was facing west. It's Friday and I'm tired from "burning the candle at both ends" this week. But it brought a smile.

Today there will be a memorial time at work for Lawrence Wisby, the building's security guard who passed away last week. I finally took time to write in his memory book in the lobby this morning as I entered the building. What I'll remember about Lawrence is his gracious greeting, always saying my name, "Good morning, Christine." [I never corrected him, i.e., it's Christina with an "a," and it somehow didn't matter.] I smiled as I remembered a colleague saying yesterday that he has a new job now working with "St. Pete" welcoming everyone into Heaven. Heaven is lucky to have him.

July 3, 2007

As I got off the train at Park Street, I remembered the excitement after work yesterday. As I was waiting for a southbound Red Line train, a man had dropped something in the rail bed. He had gotten onto the tracks using the utility steps at the end of the subway platform when an announcement over the PA speaker – confirmed by the breeze from the tunnel – alerted waiting passengers that the next train was arriving. He was walking in the direction of the train and suddenly saw it coming. It was truly like the proverbial "deer in the headlights" – he froze for what seemed like an eternity, but then turned around and started running the other way. We didn't realize that he was running toward the stairs. Some of us were screaming at him to stop so that people could lift him up. Most of us didn't know that he had used the stairs to get onto the tracks, and it looked like he was trying to outrun the train. Some of us were standing on the "yellow line" waving at the train to stop – you're supposed to stand clear of the yellow line when the train is coming, and the train usually slows down or stops when people are on the line as it approaches the platform. It seemed like forever to get the train's attention, but it finally slowed down and stopped with just the first car entering the station. A couple of MBTA officials wearing orange reflective vests appeared from somewhere and retrieved the man as he was coming up the steps from the rail bed. He appealed to them; he was desperate for whatever it was that he had dropped. One of them obliged him by going down the steps himself and retrieving what looked like his *Charlie Card* [his "T" pass] between the train track and the "third [live] rail." Tragedy averted!

Today Bob had been displaced from the Park Street Church corner to the adjacent corner of the Park Street Plaza. The roofing crew had fully overtaken the church and were assembling and storing their equipment and collateral stuff right where he used to sit. Bob was standing, leaning on his cane. We greeted each other and I gave him the gift cards. He took them with thanks saying, "I'll have food on the 4th." He said again that he hoped I realized how much he appreciated the food cards that Sue and I gave him. Jokingly, but seriously, too, I told him we weren't doing it for him, but that we were doing it for ourselves; we absolutely needed to do this. He smiled and told me about a young man who stopped by and often gave him a dollar. He said he knew somehow that it was a struggle for the man to give such a large donation. (It reminded me of the parable of the woman in the *Bible* who gave two copper coins, which was all she had, to the Temple while others just gave what they had left over.) He said that he had, on occasion, refused to take it from the young man, saying that he figured the donor needed it more.

All of a sudden, there was a swarm of hundreds of pigeons on the plaza. And there, just emerging from the Park Street Station was the woman dressed in white. Sticking to her steps like glue, they followed her over to the bench across the way. She served them their breakfast of breadcrumbs. "They have to eat, too," I remember her saying. Bob knew her. When she had disbursed the crumbs, she walked past us on her way to wherever she goes. "Good morning," I said. "Good morning," she returned with a smile. "Good morning, dear," Bob said returning a smile to her.

Then Mr. Margolis arrived and we talked briefly about the holiday coming up. "Oh, by the way," he asked Bob, "how'd you make out with Gary from Brookline?" Bob said that he was actually going to see him later in the morning. He didn't mind waiting there while the business folks were walking by as many would care enough to give him something, but the tourists just ignore him and go on their way. We suggested that he take advantage of one of the benches in the shade on Boston Common after the commuting time. He had a book to read while he was waiting. And then he asked Bob, "How are your eyes?" "Not good," he responded. I spoke up and asked if he had been able to fill out the Joslin form yet, reminding him that the sooner he got that submitted, the sooner he would be able to be considered and, hopefully, approved for free care so that he could see an ophthalmologist and any other specialist that he needed. He said he had it and he was just trying to figure out daily expenses.

Mr. Margolis asked him about the form that his doctor needed to fill out so that it could be submitted with the housing application. "Did you see your doctor yesterday, Bob?" He said that he hadn't, but that his blood pressure had been high when he checked it earlier. He tossed his finished cigarette onto the sidewalk and produced an automatic blood pressure testing device. He sat down and applied the machine to his arm and let it work out the calculations. It was something like 205 over 128. "Wow, that's high, Bob," cautioned Mr. Margolis. "Are you taking any blood pressure pills?" No, he had a patch on his chest that he said the doctor told him would be all right. I added my caution and advised him to go back to the doctor. I'm frustrated that that's all I can do.

I had been there for about 20 minutes, and it was now time to get to work. "See you next week, Bob," I said, as I was taking Thursday and Friday off from work to add to the holiday tomorrow to make a bit of a break from the routine.

As Mr. Margolis and I were leaving, the young man stopped by and gave Bob a dollar, which he took reluctantly.

July 9, 2007

As we pulled out of the Braintree station, the sparring between the "speakers" began. First we heard "ding-dong"—like at the start of a boxing match—over the loudspeaker, and then an automated, "The destination of this train is Braintree," which was answered by another "ding-dong" and a real-time, live train attendant saying, "Next stop, Quincy Adams." At Quincy Adams, the Boston-bound passengers who had just boarded scowled with befuddled looks on their faces as the automated speaker repeated, "The destination of this train is Braintree." Again, the real-time attendant automated the "ding-dong" recording over the loudspeaker and followed up with, "Next stop is Quincy Center." This continued from Quincy Center through Wollaston, North Quincy and JFK/UMASS; "ding-dong" followed by an announcement, and then "ding-dong" followed by a correction. Then the automaton changed its format and said, "Next stop, Wollaston," to which the now-much-more-frazzled T attendant replied, "Next stop, Andrew." Now, this continued through Broadway and South Station. As we left South Station for Downtown Crossing, with a surprise "left hook," the T attendant cut off the automaton's misdirected-announcement mid-sentence: "Next stop, South …" and said ["ding-dong"] "Next stop, Downtown Crossing. Change here for the Orange Line." I was glad Park Street was the next stop.

I'd been off over the long 4th of July holiday weekend and had missed my regular physical activities. My legs felt the lack of it as I reached the top step of the stairs and walked out onto the plaza.

July 10, 2007

Bob was on the Park Street Plaza this morning. He said he had gone with Mr. Jones yesterday to the Brookline Housing Authority to see about getting on the list only to find that it was a four- to five-year wait. Once again, he said, he had gotten his hopes up and, once again, they were dashed. "What about the application for the senior/disabled homeless?" I asked. "Ball's in their court," he said. It's a waiting game.

July 11, 2007

Today I traveled to Boston with my sister and two giant home-made chocolate chip cookies in a large, red Anne Klein bag. My sister was going to spend the day with the books in the Athenaeum, and it's more economical to travel to Boston together. The two cookies were for a celebration of two staff members' birthdays.

As my "luggage" [good word for it—**lug**gage] was rather heavy—the cookies were in addition to my regular sack of stuff—I suggested that we take the Green Line one stop to Government Center, which was only a couple of blocks away from my building. And I wanted to show my sister a new coffee place that I had found that overlooked Government Center Plaza near Faneuil Hall Marketplace.

I felt badly at the chance of not seeing Bob this morning, but something told me it was OK. As "chance" would have it, when we stopped at my building and I gave my sister instructions on how to get to *Borders*, where she would start the day with coffee and a new book, I ran into a co-worker with whom I had also worked on the South Shore. She was approaching the building from the other direction. She asked with a pained and questioning look on her face, which said more than the question she asked, "Are you going … tonight?" Um, well, yes, I was going to Plymouth, but I was going to a practice with my trio. Clearly, I wasn't aware of the event to which she was referring. With a very sad face she told me that a person we both knew from the area had passed away and that there was a service this evening.

Sadness, lots of sadness. I would, indeed, go tonight.

July 13, 2007

The Neponset River was exceedingly tranquil this morning. I was facing east on the train today, and it occurred to me that I don't usually see the river on the commute into town from my usual morning prospect. I wonder what else I'm missing.

Bob had reclaimed some space on the church sidewalk just outside the scaffolding and he was sitting there talking with Mr. Margolis as I approached. "Good Mornings" were shared and Bob was in better spirits today. Mr. Margolis commented that I was wearing just a casual jacket today instead of a long coat. I explained later that Friday was "casual day" at my office.

"Say, you'd better get up there to see the sand castles this weekend," urged Bob. I really would like to make an effort…maybe Sue would go with me.

"So, what's the good word this morning, Bob," I asked him. Unexpectedly, he said that he was going to say a prayer for Mr. Margolis who was going to have some kind of surgical something next week. (I don't usually ask people for details of such things.) Referring to praying, he said that's something he doesn't usually do. The expression on his face looked hopeful, full of assurance that it would work. Mr. Margolis' response was that what made it unusual was that Bob was going to pray *for him*. We all laughed.

Mr. Margolis stated and asked at the same time, "I'll see you Monday, Bob." Bob looked up at him and agreed that he would. I'm only guessing but maybe Mr. Margolis made arrangements with Bob to help him with the forms that his doctor has to sign for the application for housing.

July 16, 2007

Today a pair of pigeons entered the train waiting on the other side of the platform—just as if they were commuters themselves they walked on without hesitation. I'm not sure if they stayed for the ride though. My sister joined me today and we both laughed at the prospect of the pigeons hitching a ride to town.

"You'll get to meet Bob, today," I told my sister as we entered the Park Street plaza. He was sitting on the corner outside the church, just in front of the scaffolding; there was enough room. I introduced them and she commented on the Michael Crichton paperback lying [inside-pages-down] open and spine up holding Bob's place. Crichton is one of her favorite authors. He enjoyed the author, too. We dropped a few of his book titles in discussion.

Bob asked for a sand castle report, to which I had to reply that, after a valiant effort, my car ended up breaking something (we think it's a strut that rusted out) and it's in the car hospital. So, sad to say, I never made it.

Mr. Margolis then appeared with a brace on his forearm and hand—one that you might wear for carpal tunnel syndrome. I introduced him to my sister, after which he asked me for a sand castle report as well; I related my sad tale.

I made some insensitive comment about the brace on his arm, referring to it as a common occurrence (it was the third such time I'd seen one of his arms bound after some mishap). I didn't realize how insensitive I had been until the words were out of my mouth. I thought that maybe I could blame it on my sister's presence and influence as we often chuck comments back and forth in a playful sisterly way. But, no, the words came out of my mouth.

It was getting to be time to go. I handed Bob our gift cards and some extra cash from our friend, Lee, who was back for a summer visit from Florida.

Bob asked me to thank Sue and Lee as we said good-bye. Mr. Margolis reminded Bob about the papers for his doctor's signature and then joined us on our way down Tremont Street.

Later on after I got to work, I quickly sent an e-mail apologizing for the insensitivity of my remark (I had forgotten that he had injured himself last week on the boat.) I told him that I wanted to blame it on my sister, etc., etc., etc., but the fault was indeed mine alone.

He wrote back later that morning, using "LOL" at the beginning of his note. "Hmmm," I thought. "What in the world could that stand for?" It was a new language to me and I finally had to ask one of the younger staff members what it meant and she laughed and said it meant "laughing out loud"—it was a text message abbreviation. When I got home I asked my sister about it and she verified that I'd been hiding under a rock much too long and that, yes, there was this whole new language of abbreviations people use to do text messaging.

WELL [that's the word, "well," said in somewhat of an exclamatory fashion and not something that stands for four other words], this experience had to be captured in song as I "L'd OL" at myself for being such an antique. I've been called a Luddite (defined by *Word Perfect's* dictionary as "a person opposed to industrialization or new technology") by many – indeed the fellows in my musical trio were stunned when I told them I now had a cell phone (after knowing me for three years or so). I just kept an old one—the one that looks like a box—in the glove compartment of my car and doesn't work unless you plug it into the cigarette lighter and the car's engine has to be running—just in case of an emergency.

What Kind of Rube Am I?

What kind of rube am I, who never learned to text?
It seems that I'm the only one who never learned this alphabet.
What kind of phone is this—flip or clam shell!?
A phony cell in which your every thought might dwell?
WH5 words like these? They make me SIS.
What me try? Well, you'd just ROTFLUTS!
But, BTW, I just don't give a damn!
@TEOTD, a true Luddite I am!

July 17, 2007

As I was getting ready for work this morning, I was thinking about some of the songs that our trio might do for an upcoming gig. I remembered "Right Field" about a self-conscious kid who was always picked last when the kids in the neighborhood were putting together baseball teams, and how he always wound up in right field. I thought about how my dad told me I threw [a ball] "like a girl" whenever he played catch with my brother and me. I thought about how my parents' generation had a preference for males . . . for example, when money was tight, my brother got to stay in college, but I couldn't because "he'll have to support a family when he grows up."

I'm not sure much has really changed. I remembered about how a young teenager in El Salvador told us just a few years ago how her mother preferred her brothers over her and how that impacted her life; she was never affirmed or fully valued. In that country the campesinos living in the mountains intentionally let their boy toddlers run around in shirts but with bare bottoms showing so you will see that they have a boy.

Anyway, "Right Field" reminded me about the awful ballroom dancing classes as a young girl—sixth grade I think it was. There were 23 kids in the class that met Friday nights for what seemed like weeks on end! There were 10 boys and 11 girls; talk about poor planning! I was always the 11th girl—A.K.A. the wall flower. The teacher took pity on me and danced with me as I recall. I didn't learn much except that I was pitiable.

As I thought about all of this, my thoughts turned into a rhyme as the beginning of a new song. I wrote the words on the train this morning and "attached" them to a tune that I kept singing over and over in my head so I could plant it there and not forget. When I got to work I called my cell phone from my phone at work to sing and record the chorus of the song—which was all that I had so far—into voice mail so I wouldn't forget (I've learned that if you want to remember something [at this age], you've got to record it and/or write it down! Otherwise it's gone!) My "message will be kept for 14 days" on my cell, which is more than I'll need as when I get home I'll play it into my tape recorder for safe keeping. I wanted to call my home phone to leave the "message," but I'd wake up my sister who is sleeping in today after a restless night.

> *Dance, little wall flower, up on your toes!*
> *You can still dance in your second-hand clothes.*
> *Soon you'll be wearing fine buttons and bows.*
> *Won't you dance, little wall flower? Dance!*

Now I'll be "listening" all day for the words to the verses. But I also have some questions: What does the "wall flower" actually represent? What do the "second-hand clothes" symbolize? What kind of "dance" is it? What's so bad about dancing alone? What is the meaning of "fine satin and bows"? Who's singing the song anyway?

July 18, 2007

Another restless night and an early (2:30 a.m.) morning. Well, at least it was productive; I finished the song that I had started yesterday. "Buttons" changed to "satin," and it occurred to me that it might symbolize the story of *Esther*.

> *Wall Flower*
>
> *Dance, little wall flower, up on your toes.*
> *You can still dance in your second-hand clothes.*
> *But, I see you wearing fine satin and bows!*
> *Won't you dance, little wall flower? Dance!*

Dance, little wall flower! You have a choice.
Someone is asking and you know the voice.
Answer it well and there's cause to rejoice!
Come on, dance, little wall flower! Dance!

Don't be afraid little wall flower, dance on your own.
See, I'll be your partner; you'll not dance alone.
"Is this not the time ..." not for this you were grown?
Go on, dance, little wall flower! Dance!

It's time, little wall flower, kick up your heels.
Yes, you're afraid, and I know how that feels.
But there is nothing that Love cannot heal.
Time to dance, little wall flower! Dance!
Take the chance, little flower! Let's dance!

Continuing the metaphor, changing its rhythm, the song ends with the first verse and chorus of "Lord of the Dance."

Bob was sitting on a small, portable, metal-and-green-canvas stool on his corner this morning reading another book. "I devour them," he said. He took his cane and stood up while we talked. He was concerned about Mr. Margolis as he had his surgery yesterday ... we agreed to keep him in our thoughts and prayers. Bob thought he might call him at his office later on to see if there was any news.

He asked how my sister did in town the other day and I told him she enjoyed going to the Athenaeum and that a great aunt of ours used to work there years ago. He mentioned that he had an acquaintance who was a reference librarian and she often stopped by with leftovers from the night before on her way to work. She was on vacation this week so she wasn't around. But we agreed that we couldn't imagine how much information they [reference librarians] must have in their heads ... and it was more than we could imagine. He mentioned that he knew a fellow—I think he said it was when he was at the University of Southern Florida – who was a medical reference librarian, and that was something we couldn't fathom either. Bob said that he taught people – and I think the librarian was one of them – how to do repairs on their cars while he was in Florida. I said that I could never do anything with my car, citing the recent malfunction over the weekend, which turned out to be a broken strut, two of which (along with some other gadgets) had to be replaced for eight hundred dollars and change. Bob grimaced when I told him. While he was a good teacher (he said and I believe), I said that, no matter how good a teacher he might be, I am not a good student when it comes to mechanical things. I said that I could write music and play the guitar and that was my "thing." Bob's was to teach auto repair. The librarian had yet another gift. We agreed that we all have different gifts and we could appreciate each other for them.

I told him that I was glad he was here this morning as I'd be at a meeting most of the day in Plymouth tomorrow and then was taking Friday off. I wished him well and he asked after my friend, Sue. She was having her eye surgery today and we agreed to keep her in our thoughts and prayers today, too.

July 23, 2007

A plethora of full-length parasols "s'il pleu" today. (That's probably not the correct spelling or tense of the French for "if it's raining" – I'll check later with my French-fluent niece.) There were four umbrellas that accompanied passengers onto the train this morning. One black-and-white striped one was held by a middle-aged man in a summer-weight tan suit and twitched (the umbrella, not the man) precariously close to my face while its owner adjusted his bag and stance as he settled into reading a book called "Future Girl," which was illustrated with a cartoon of a girl seeming to paddle a coffin. Maybe that's not what it was, but that's what I caught out of my eye. My umbrella, the collapsible kind, was tucked in my tote bag, readily accessible should the sky open up when I walk out on to Park Street plaza. I have a full-length black one, too, at home that I use when I act as "Mary Poppins" when I do one of my children's programs.

Well, it wasn't raining yet – just threatening to. Bob wasn't there, but it's Monday. As I walked across the street I saw a huge sign, hung to enclose the wall-to-wall scaffolding on the broad side of the church, saying that Park Street Church was celebrating 200 years. Guess it was getting spiffed up for its birthday.

Walking past the church, I spied out of the corner of my eye a man in jeans, maybe in his 40's, standing/leaning against the wall in front of the cemetery.

He had a paper cup in his hand and he asked softly with a furrowed brow and sad eyes, "Can you spare some change?" I averted my eyes and walked past. Not too many steps further, I said, "Turn around and give him something." I stopped fished around in my purse for a dollar, turned around and he was gone. Hmmm. It felt like a movie when one minute you see the angel and then, in a twinkling, you don't. I didn't get a second chance this time. When *will* I learn? I continued walking down Tremont Street and handed the dollar to another fellow sitting on the sidewalk further down in front of the cemetery. He was grateful.

July 25, 2007

As I took my seat on the train, I looked up and there was this horrific picture advertising a new movie, (Skin something … I don't want to even remember the title or put the description of the picture in words lest I say it and unleash some demonic spirit). Don't they know there are young children with their families who ride the "T" every day? I'm sure seeing it would be traumatic to a child; it did a number on me. I averted my eyes and got lost in my thoughts. Maybe I'll write them a letter. Maybe not, as I now remember that it's been nine months since I submitted a form for a refund from the "T's" administration office in Charlestown after I purchased the wrong "T" pass in October last year. It said on the form to allow a few weeks for processing. I called them in December to see when I could expect it and the man I spoke with said they were still working on July's refunds. Still nothing. Hmmm.

A busy morning … an extra element today in bringing a homemade, gargantuan designer chocolate chip cookie to work, commissioned by one of my workmates who's giving it to some friends who are going to have a baby boy. I brought stuff to decorate it at work as it would be impossible to carry on the "T." While, I hadn't seen Bob for the last two days and wanted to get his food cards to him, it was also hard to carry all of my stuff – it was cumbersome. I decided anyway to get off at Park Street as usual and go up to the plaza to see if he was there. He wasn't, but I'm glad I checked; it would have bothered me if he was there and I bypassed him – all because of a cookie. So I went back downstairs at Park Street to catch the Green Line north to Government Center.

July 30, 2007

On my way to the "T" this morning, just after I merged onto Route 3 North in Weymouth, against the backdrop of a quickly darkening sky and distant lightening, an illuminated construction sign read: "Blasting ahead. Be prepared to stop." The warning came none too soon as a split second later, nature blasted the sky open with thunder and lightening, releasing torrents of rain. I clicked the windshield wipers to full blast.

After I had parked the car in the "shelter" of the garage, the storm drains started overflowing onto the parking garage floor; water was surging from them horizontally throughout the lower level where I usually park. As I was getting ready to leave the car, what had been dry ground where I had originally parked, was being consumed by an incoming tide. I started the car up again and looked for higher ground. (You'd think they would have engineered the pipes so that the overflow water would go out of the garage, not into it!) I would need my heavy duty "Mary Poppins" umbrella today for sure!

July 31, 2007

At the Quincy Center stop, an avalanche of bodies tumbled down the stairs to board the train before the doors closed. The doors show no mercy. An elderly man shuffled down the stairs at the tail end of the crowd and made it to the train just as the doors were closing. It's a hostile world.
The advertisement for the *Charlie Card* on the wall at the station reminded me again that I hadn't received my refund *from last October.* Maybe I'll send them a song to [humorously?] remind them … it would be entitled "The Massachusetts Bay Transportation Authority Refund Policy Protest Song" – a takeoff on the "Metropolitan Transit Authority Protest Song," made popular by the *Kingston Trio* in the 60's, (or "Charlie on the MTA").
Bob wasn't there this morning … I hope to see him tomorrow.
August 3, 2007

It was a breeze to get to the "T" this morning; traffic was very light on this Friday in August. I thought about it being a popular vacation time of year, which also made me think that there are just four weeks left before the roads would be busy again with school back in session and the [out-of-the-home] workforce in full force. The at-home work force never actually gets a vacation.

Today a thirty-ish man boarded the train with a solitary golf club—specifically, a putter. He sat on the end seat across from me and tried to prop it up against the railing next to him. It wouldn't stand right-side-up, so he flipped it up-side-down, and the way the shank was curved at the end allowed it to fit just perfectly under and around the railing. There it stood, up-side-down for the ride into town.

Over him sat the sign from *ITA Software*: "Solve This…Work Here." The "this" part of the message was: "How long a chain of overlapping movie titles, like 'Live and Let Die Another Day of the Dead Poets Society,' can you find?"

Someone had written next to it "little.too.much.time.on.your.hands.com?"

As I left the train at Park Street, I noticed new electronic message signs had been installed on the platform—I think there were four of them. I thought, "Gee, I don't want to begrudge them their new, fancy doo-dads, but wouldn't it be nice if they took care of things, like hiring enough staff back in Chelsea to process backlogged refunds from customers, who submitted their refund requests almost a year ago, first before they bought any new toys?" All the signs told us was that if we wanted schedule information we could go to their website for it. That's it. You could put that on a paper sign for a fraction of the cost of the new ones plus the electricity it will take to run them. Then I remembered the conversation on NPR this morning about the bridge in Minnesota that collapsed this week; they were talking about how there's never enough money [or interest, to be more truthful] to do "maintenance" on roads and bridges, but we love to build big [dig] new ones. No mending of buildings or systems. I suppose that could apply to relationships, too. [Hmmm, seems a theme is emerging here.] And I am humbled to think about so many couples I know who have stuck it out together—for better, for worse. Humbling, indeed.

No sign of Bob for a fortnight now, so I'll hold my two weeks' worth of gift cards in the hope that I'll see him next week. I wanted to let him know that our trio was going to be singing for the "Common Cathedral" on Boston Common on Sunday … maybe he'll come.

August 06, 2007

Park Street Plaza had such a different energy yesterday, Sunday, when our trio played for the "Common Cathedral" service held there at the fountain. Week in and week out for years there has been an outdoor worship service organized by Ecclesia Ministries for the Park Street angels. About 50 participated all together, but another 100 or so sat in the periphery; they all, however, wound up standing in line for lunch after the service.

There was a segment during the service when, within the circle of worshipers, people could express a joy or concern. A man named John (who Bob knew from a rehab shelter) was there. He was dressed in a plaid shirt and shorts, and in his gruff voice he said that he had been in jail for 26 days and that he was grateful to be out. Other concerns were voiced including one woman's whose sister was suffering with pneumonia. At the end of that segment we sang happy birthday or happy anniversary to people who were celebrating another day of sobriety. Later on as the service continued, John could be found across the way under a tree near an exhibit of pictures of "Auschwitz in China" and a man playing *Jesu, Joy of Man's Desiring* on a flute. He addressed the crowds of tourists milling about, saying, "Does anybody have a dollar so I can get some food?"

Choices.

There was a police officer on Bob's corner this morning. Bob wasn't there. This will be week three.

August 8, 2007

Today my concern about Bob got the better of me which launched a series of e-mails back and forth between Jonathan and myself. "He's gone missing before," he reminded me. This I knew. He thought it would be a good idea, though, to make a call to the Revere police to see if he could find anything out. They directed him to the *Shipwreck Lounge*; an upstairs room of said lounge is where he lived. He made a call and learned that folks there knew of Bob, and they knew at least that he wasn't dead. He asked the woman with whom he spoke to pass the word that Bob's friends were asking after him. He reminded me also that Bob suffered from depression and that it may be that he was just too down to make the trip in to town. He seemed sure that if Bob was in the hospital that he'd call one of us.

I thought about seeing if I could arrange for the *Pea Pod* delivery service to get some food to him and I called the *Shipwreck* to see if they might let me know the address. While she knew of Bob, the lady I spoke with couldn't help me and suggested that I call back Saturday morning.

Frustration. A dead end.

August 10, 2007

An email today from Jonathan said: "I just got a message from Bob that he's in the ER at MGH and will call back when he can. His voice sounded strong on the voicemail."

Hope. Thanks.

August 14, 2007

When I arrived at work this morning there was a phone message waiting for me. It was a call from Bob on Monday, which I had taken off, so I was concerned that I was late in retrieving it. He said he was in Mass. General and that he had been there several days ... he didn't know when he got there. He thought that he might be leaving [Monday] but wasn't sure. Quickly I called the hospital and they connected me with his room. He was still there.

He told me he was suffering from foot problems and anemia now on top of everything else. I asked him if he had talked with the social worker there to talk about what his options were with services in his community and possible next steps. He said he would. I asked if he would be there later around lunchtime as I could walk over and drop off the food cards that I as collecting. He said he thought he would, and then emphasized that he would indeed be there and would wait for me even if he were released earlier. I asked if I could get him anything that he needed right away and he asked for a pack of cigarettes. I told him it was the one thing that I could not do for him. He faked crying—which, for a moment, I wasn't so sure was put on—as he hadn't had a smoke in days. Then he turned off the "act" as quickly as he assumed it and said that was OK and he understood. (I still put in some extra cash in the envelope with the food cards so he could buy them if he absolutely had to.)

When I arrived he was dressed and sitting on the bed with a social worker sitting next to him on the phone talking to a lady who would arrange food stamps for him. She handed the phone over to him so he answered her questions for the application. They got cut off and so had to redial and reopen the discussion. While the social worker was speaking on the phone, Bob and I chatted briefly. They wanted him to go to the Sarah McGinnis House, where he had gone before when he had broken his leg. But he refused. Anyway, they were trying to get him a wheelchair, so that would help to make him more ambulatory, and comfortable in being so.

He also told me, adding more insult to more injury, that one day a few weeks ago that, when he was doing all of his laundry, *all of his laundry* – clothes as well as blankets and sheets, etc. – in the laundromat, he filled up three washers and then went out for coffee to wait for it to get done. When he returned, the laundry, together with the shopping cart he had acquired to transport it, was gone.

He got back on the phone and was then put on hold for a minute. While he was waiting, he said thanks for everything and that he'd see me tomorrow as he expected that he would be on the call for a while and didn't want to make me wait.

As I was walking back to my office, I forgot to tell him that I wouldn't be working in town tomorrow. It would have to be Thursday.

August 16, 2007

Thursday it was. As my sister and I came out of the escalated exit across Tremont Street, I was so happy to see Bob speaking to Jonathan on the corner. Bob was sitting in a brand new wheel chair. He had socks and specially designed sandals [for diabetics he said] on his feet which made him much more comfortable. We talked for 10 minutes or so about his ordeal. He had been bedridden for four or five days and finally had to crawl out to the pay phone outside to call 911. He was lying on the sidewalk when the ambulance came to pick him up; he just couldn't stand.

Jonathan finished up by saying that he would still work on the housing application form for Hearth, which he explained was the former Coalition to End Elder Homelessness, and I offered that the application for Joslin Clinic would take about a month to process. We continue to hope.

We said goodbye for now and left Bob to greet the Thursday regulars. As we walked down Tremont Street, Jonathan remembered he had forgotten to speak to him about something and needed to go back. He also asked about getting Bob a phone. I told him my friend, Sue, and I "were on it today." There would be no more procrastination on my part. I can't stand it that Bob wasn't able to call for help when he needed it; this was something that could be fixed.

August 17, 2007

I purchased the phone yesterday and brought it to work today hoping to give it to Bob, but he wasn't on the corner. Jonathan had mentioned that Bob oftentimes is off Fridays if he takes in enough on Thursdays, but that he goes there a lot on Sundays. Maybe I'll take Sue to meet him then at the Park Street Church so she can give him the phone herself—maybe as an early birthday present. August 31 is coming up fast.

August 24, 2007

There were three people including me in the end car of the train as we left Braintree. Maybe it's because it's Friday and the beginning of the last weekend before Labor Day. Maybe it's because there was an accident on the expressway just south of where I get on. Maybe it's because two trains left the station in the time it took me to drive into the parking garage, take my ticket, park and then walk to the platform. Maybe it's just *because*; it doesn't need a reason.

A friend boarded at the North Quincy stop … it's always surprising, but I don't know why, to see someone you know on the "T." I usually just feel so anonymous. Anyway, we spoke about maybe getting together later in the evening to go to a local coffee house as a songwriter friend was featuring there tonight. I'll decide later … it's been a very long and somewhat sleep-deprived week for me. He went on to Haymarket on the Green Line and I walked up the stairs to the plaza above.

Bob was there on the corner near the church in his wheelchair this morning. He was tired, too, but all things considered, he was OK. He was full of stories about the earlier days, travels to North Dakota, Montana, and Mexico and of living in Chicago where he started a candy business. It did very well; it kept him in BMW motorcycles—a new one each year. I urged him again to write the stories; they're all about *just plain life*. Besides, it would help me connect the dots of his life. I don't know why I need to know; I'm just curious, interested.

Then he pulled out an envelope with a form letter that he had received from the agency to which he had applied for food stamps. It stated that he was not eligible for benefits through that agency, but that he could contact them for further information. *What*?! Does that mean he needs to go to another agency to get the benefits, maybe one that serves Revere? Is he to receive benefits through MassHealth? And if he's not eligible, *who is*!?

Could I help make a phone call and pursue it for him? I asked. No, he would rather go to the agency and speak to them face-to-face. He will do that today.

Frustration.

We spoke of our respective and similar weekend plans, which were to just hang out and be—just *be*. It was getting late and I had to be on my way.

August 27, 2007

A "Luke Danes" (a character on the *Gilmore Girls*) look-alike sat across from me this morning on the "T." He was wearing a long-sleeve plaid shirt and khaki slacks, and peered at his laptop through dark sunglasses. Such coordination and concentration – I don't know if I could balance a laptop on my lap, type and think at the same time!

On the plaza at Park Street the lady in white with the beautiful, gentle spirit walked over to the usual spot and scattered seed on the pavement for the birds. They began to flock around her and I smiled as I watched. She caught me watching and waved. I waved back. My smile continued.

Looking across the street to Bob's corner, I saw that he wasn't there, but there was a big sign attached to the scaffolding near where he usually stands. It said, "Happy Birthday, Bob! We Love You!" Perhaps it was from the folks at church yesterday ... I hope it stays up all week for his big day on Friday.

August 28, 2007

I received an e-mail from Mr. Margolis this morning saying that he hadn't seen Bob on Tuesday. But he related that on Sunday afternoon he received a call from a guy who had found Bob's phone on the beach. He had asked the man to bring it to the Shipwreck for them to get it to Bob. But he wanted a reward. He had called Bob's phone this morning to see if he had returned it, but the guy who answered wasn't Bob. The unknown voice told him he had the wrong number, which, he said, wasn't true, and that he was pretty sure it was the guy who called on Sunday. He suggested I cancel the pre-paid plan so he couldn't use the phone; maybe the guy would think again about bringing it back to Bob. Luckily we bought a pay-as-you-go plan and there wasn't much time on it ... but I'll cancel whatever is left.

I agreed with Mr. Margolis: "Frustrating—or maybe infuriating—isn't it?

August 29, 2007

A familiar voice in a summer chapeau walked up beside me on Tremont Street: "I thought that was you." Jonathan and I walked as we chatted, still frustrated at Bob's dilemma with the phone. We agreed that "stuff" happens, but it seemed to happen more to someone like Bob. Jonathan wondered if he should remind Bob again that "God helps those who help themselves." While I remembered hearing once that that phrase doesn't actually exist in the *Bible*—that it is more of a human convention—instead I related that, once upon a time, a very long time ago, a man was asked, "Do you want to be healed?" [of his paralysis of 38 years]. The man made the excuse that no one helped him into the pool when the [healing] waters were stirred. He wasn't listening. He didn't hear the question. He never said "yes." He just made excuses. (What would "yes" mean anyway?)

I think that God *does* try to help those who can't seem to help themselves—through the hearts and hands of other people.

These Hands

I have hands to play the music
so this heart of mine can hear,
and these hands can sign the language
of the one with silent ear.
I have hands to feed the hungry,
and hands to clothe the poor,
and these hands can greet the stranger
as she knocks at my door.

I have hands to hold the hammer,
and hands to guide the plow,
and these hands can thread the needle,
though my eyes are tired now.
I have hands to hold the baby
as he suckles at the breast,
and these hands console the dying
as they find their final rest.

I have hands to write the letter,
and hands to wash their feet,
and these hands can hold the child
whose home is in the street.
I have hands to grind the flour,
and hands to knead the bread,
and these hands can share the harvest
of a life that once was dead.

I have hands to tend the garden,
and hands to sow the seed,
and these hands can spread the bounty
to a universe in need.
I have hands to weave the linen
from the threads of finest gold,
and these hands can mend the broken,
wipe the tear — heal a soul.

In parting, and in error, I reminded him that it was Bob's birthday tomorrow (it's the 31st not the 30th). When I got to my office, I dashed off an e-mail message to make the correction. He advised that if we were going to do anything for Bob's birthday, it should probably be done tomorrow anyway – Thursday – as he wasn't sure if Bob would get to Park Street Church on Friday.

August 30, 2007

Rats. It's Thursday, and no sign of Bob anywhere. He hasn't been here all week. I'm concerned again because of Jonathan's e-mail yesterday that said he had received a phone message from Bob [not from his own phone]. He said he sounded very tired, but that he would try to get out on Thursday. I hope I'll see him tomorrow … maybe tomorrow. He'll mark his 58th birthday tomorrow.

Between August and October, Bob had had several long confinements at Massachusetts General Hospital—a kidney infection that required a second admission and further complications from diabetes affecting his feet. Each time, several days or weeks would go by before he was able to contact Mr. Margolis to let him know he was there. Communicating via e-mail, Jonathan would let me know Bob's whereabouts, and we took turns visiting him at the hospital after work.

Messages to me from Jonathan …

September 19, 2007

"…Bob and I spent the morning at Ruggles House … the people there were VERY nice and caring. The nurse and social worker who did the evaluation had to work hard to get Bob to admit that he does need assistance…finally he caught on and as the interview progressed it became clear that he really needs assistance with medication; the form that the doctor filled out for his medications was markedly different from the prescriptions that he is actually getting. He's had no help in trying to gauge how much insulin he needs, etc., etc.

"There are only one or two apartments (single room, counter with sink, microwave and small refrigerator and bath, but all clean and neat) now available and other people on the list. They first have to get Bob approved, probably at a meeting next Monday. Then they need to get the response from the CORI inquiry and from an agency that provides elder foster care or something which pays for the services (i.e., not rent I gather)."

October 4, 2007

"Good news, but…

"Got a call yesterday from the woman who runs the assisted living that the property manager was figuring out what Bob would have to put up as a security deposit, apparently, the last step. Got a message from her that she has the amount. Sounds like they have a room for him. The problem – no Bob. I take it you have not spoken to him."

And then later…

"I got a call from Ruggles Assisted Living – they're ready for him to move in immediately! Now I just have to find him."

October 5, 2007

"Further developments: I got another call from Ruggles Assisted Living – they were ready for him to move in yesterday! Called the Shipwreck just, lo and behold, as he was just coming in. Spoke to him and we agreed on Monday. Called back to arrange that with Ruggles…I'm not certain about him remembering for Monday. BUT he was VERY excited…"

Epilogue

December 5, 2007

At precisely five o'clock the carillon in the newly refurbished steeple of the Park Street Church rang out with "Oh Come, All Ye Faithful." On a colder-than-usual day in early December, snow had been falling since mid-afternoon. It created a sense of magic and anticipation in the evening air as it sparkled to the ground—like *Peter Pan's Tinker Bell* sprinkling fairy dust on the parade of weary holiday shoppers and evening commuters. Now on my way home, my footsteps were slow and deliberate as I navigated the icy brick sidewalk outside the church. I glanced over at the spot on the corner where Bob sits, and I remembered our conversations over the last few weeks.

"Ya know," Bob shared recently, "I wake up at night now and I'm in a bed with clean sheets and it's warm, and I still can't get used to it. But, my laundry is done and they wash my dishes, too."

But he's been having trouble calling it "home" and he hopes that they don't kick him out.

Trying to provide a bit of encouragement, I shared with him [rather insensitively, now that I think about it] that as I get older, "home" isn't so much of a place to me anymore as it is a feeling of being grounded, on a firm and stable foundation. He allowed that, while what I said was very poetic, since he never had that sense of security within a family or a consistent physical structure—a safe harbor to protect him from the elements—my ill-conceived effort to prop up his spirits didn't hold much weight. Embarrassed at the words that had just come out of my mouth, I agreed that it shouldn't and apologized for lapsing into a temporary state of ignorance of his perspective and "the lenses through which he viewed the world."

Perspective: *"A mental view of the relationship of aspects of a subject to each other and to a whole"* (Webster). Contemplating differences in "perspectives" as they relate to my earlier comments about toes, my life experience allows me to see them as whimsical if not silly (to wit, the song "Toes"). Mine are intact, healthy and pretty much taken for granted until I stub one. For

someone living [mostly] on [and intermittently off] the streets in the winter—
especially someone with diabetes whose extremities are compromised to begin
with—his experience is one of pain and loss of function, if they are not lost
altogether. It fosters depression and fear for his ability to maintain his health
and independence. His are, indeed, quite a different set of lenses.

Further [comparing and contrasting], I remember once, when preparing for
my first work-study trip to El Salvador, some of us were thinking about toys
we might bring to the children. Remembering a game that I played with my
brothers and sisters as a child when visiting my grandparents, I suggested we
make bean bags and a target—a clown's face painted on a wide wooden board
with an opening for his mouth—through which the bags could be tossed.
Mortified yet again, it was explained to me by the work-study organizers that
this would be disrespectful to the people; they subsisted on corn, prepared in
various ways, and beans—and not many of them at that. The precious beans
used to fill one bean bag might be all they had for one day. And it just occurred
to me: buying wood for the target would be an absurd extravagance.

Another memory from *Race and Class in Human Services* at UMASS Boston:
for the "walking in someone else's shoes" [or absence thereof in this case]
assignment, a fellow [WASP, middle-class] classmate was assigned the role
of a homeless black man in Boston whose life experience he was required to
mentally, compassionately (defined as "suffering with") "try on" and record in
a journal for two weeks; this was after his comment to the professor that "they
all should just pull themselves up by their bootstraps." He was to live as one
who had no boots in a culture where racism – as much as we'd like to think
we've evolved beyond it – is still alive and well.

During the first several weeks of moving into his new quarters, when he wasn't
out at Park Street, Bob stayed pretty much to himself. But after a while he
told me that he joined in an evening game of BINGO with a group of his new
neighbors in their common living area. He shared that, now that he doesn't
have to worry about daily survival, he has started thinking about where and
how he might do his copper craft work or paint lighthouses on slate. He's
taking things one day at a time.

Sue and I have continued to provide him with the supermarket gift cards as he has the option of cooking for himself in his own apartment. The Silver Line bus that he takes from his apartment building to Park Street goes right by the Stop & Shop a few blocks away. Making use of the common kitchen area, he once surprised everyone with his skill in baking a blueberry pie, which he shared with the residents and staff. And now it's easier for him to "commute" via the Silver Line bus to Park Street and the church where he often still sits and reads a paperback book and greets "the regulars"—especially the children. He said he missed seeing them. But now he only places one sign on the sidewalk next to him that admonishes all to obey the law and "smile." Isn't that just the kind of thing an angel would say?

December 25, 2007

I was reading recently about "synchronicity" in Gregg Levoy's *Callings*.

> *... Jung believed that synchronicities mirror deep psychological processes, carry messages the way dreams do, and take on meaning and provide guidance to the degree that they correspond to emotional states and inner experiences – to thoughts, feelings, visions, dreams and premonitions. For example ... you're worried about the isolation of moving to a small town, worried that you'll be bored for lack of stimulation, wondering how you'll cope without a decent coffeehouse and the ability to get a pizza at 2 a.m., and a few days before leaving, while out on a hike miles from anywhere, you find a fortune cookie message: "You discover pleasure in your own company, and rely on your mind to occupy you."*

I remembered Bob's fortune cookie that said in the next year he'd have a new home.

Part II

While this is where my journal ended, the story continued. Finding housing for Bob was not to be the end. Sue and Jonathan, my son and I continued to visit him in his new digs – sometimes for holidays, sometimes for no particular reason. During our visits Ruggles' staff would come in bringing his medicine and check to see if he needed anything. They would also wash any dishes he had, and take care of his cleaning and laundry, too. In spite of this new, secure living arrangement, he never felt totally safe and made a point of always sitting on the side of his bed or in a chair facing the door, so that he wouldn't have to watch out for anyone coming up behind him.

"Good morning, Mr. Wright," said Sarah, one of the nurses as she knocked and entered the room during one of our visits. "I'm dropping off your meds for today. I'll leave them here on the counter."

Bob responded, "Mornin' Sarah. Thanks."

Sarah continued, "Oh, and the van will be here to pick you up to go for your appointment in about 30 minutes. Is there anything you need before I go?"

"No, thank you kindly," said Bob. Got everything I need."

In early October 2008 I had some hard news to share with Bob. He had ventured into town this particular day, and I met him on his corner at the Park Street Church. Just a few days before, I had learned that our friend, Sue, had passed away.

"Hey, Bob...how goes it today?" I said as I approached him.

"Ugh...my feet hurt," he said and lit a cigarette. (Irony noted.) Just then one of his friends walked up to him looking for a match. It took him a number of tries to light it since the wind was so strong that day and kept blowing out each match he lit. He finally succeeded and the fellow walked away.

"Hey, Bob," I continued, "I have some hard news that I have to tell you."

"Yeah?" he responded suspiciously. "What is it?"

"Sue's been pretty sick lately," I started. "She didn't let a lot of people know about it. I guess she wanted to live life on her own terms. She had had cancer some 30 years ago and said the treatment she had for it was really horrific. She hasn't gone back to a doctor since. But, she said she made a bargain with God to let her live long enough to see her children grow up. Her kids are all married now, and some have kids of their own. So I guess that's just what she did. She'd been ill for a couple of weeks and then finally went to the hospital over the weekend. She died on Monday," I concluded cautiously.

Outraged at the news, Bob stood up and, leaning on his cane, walked around and whipped his arm in the air as if punching it. "Shit...see...everyone keeps leaving me!" he yelled. "They all leave me! They just leave me! You can't trust anyone...! Shit...they just leave me."

Interrupting him, and trying to deescalate his rage, I said, "Bob!! Bob, listen! She didn't die to leave you! She was very, very sick. She didn't do it to leave you. She was just very sick."

Bob calmed down a bit, sat down and lit another cigarette. "Yeah...OK," he said as he took a drag. Yeah...OK."

Later that year I received some hard news of my own. It was a Wednesday, Christmas Eve day. I was in a treatment room at the hospital sitting on an exam table, accompanied by a close friend, to find out the results of a recent biopsy. I should have been more suspicious; with prior biopsies they called me on the phone to say that everything was fine. This time they wanted to give me the news in person. While a nurse stood by, the doctor entered the room carrying my chart and put it down on the counter. Putting his hand on my shoulder, he announced the verdict.

"Christina," he said directly, but with compassion, "this is breast cancer."

I was stunned and burst into tears, and was immediately consoled by my friend.

He continued, "We discussed the case at yesterday's tumor board. The cancer is contained, and while there's an outside chance we may be able to treat it successfully with a lumpectomy and radiation, we all feel the most effective treatment needs to be a total mastectomy. It's because of how extensive it is and where's it's located. My colleague at Faulkner has agreed that this would be the best treatment for your cancer."

As I tried to regain some composure (as it is my practice not to deal with anger very directly, if at all), I asked, "OK, so what do I do...I need to know what this is, I need to know all I can about it ... and ... what can I do?"

The next day, later in the morning on Christmas day, my son and I kept our plans to visit Bob at his apartment. When we arrived Jonathan was already there, and Bob had the NASA channel on the TV. We gave Bob a DVD player and some DVDs that we purchased together as a gift for him. I also brought him a homemade turkey dinner which he put in the refrigerator for later. We sat down, and after we visited for a while, I told Bob and Jonathan the news.

I started, "OK...so...there's never a good time to tell you this, but I need to tell you both. I just learned that I have breast cancer and..."

Visibly angry, Bob erupted and started yelling at the world: "See what did I tell you – they always leave me! What did I..."

This time I interrupted him. Leaning over in my chair to reach out to him, I said, "Bob! Listen, Bob! Bob, I'm not going anywhere. I'm still going to be here. I'm not going anywhere."

Bob calmed down some and realized what he said.

"The doctor said it's early and it's treatable," I continued, "but I have to be home for a while after the surgery – like six weeks or so. But we can talk on the phone, and I'll write, too," I reassured.

Picking up a jacket, Bob said, "Yeah...OK. I need a cigarette. Let's go out back."

We all went out to the patio in the back so Bob could smoke. It was a warm December day, and we sat outside until he finished his smoke. Laughing at the silly antics of the cat that lives outside in a make-shift cardboard box shelter helped us release the tension.

After a while, I said to Bob, "Well, we need to get going. I'll be around during January if you're still going to Park Street; I can see you then. But you can also call...you have my number."

"Yeah," Bob said. "And I'm still going to the church. It's actually easy to get there on the Silver Line bus from here. It's not for the same reason anymore, but I really miss the kids and the *regulars*. I gotta see 'em."

Jonathan and I kept in touch with him in the weeks after my surgery. We spoke on the phone a couple of times and I sent some notes, too. He had this wonderful way of displaying cards that he had received from Sue – and now mine as well – on two rawhide shoe laces that hung from a couple of nails on the wall in his apartment.

In June Bob had to be seen more frequently because of the damage to his kidneys caused by diabetes that had been uncontrolled over so many years. A van from Ruggles would take him to and from the health center for his appointments and tests. He took them in stride – a necessary evil.

Then during an appointment one day in August, his doctor began, "Mr. Wright I wish I could give you better news, but the fact of the matter is that your kidneys are no longer functioning as they should. I know we've talked about this before as a possible complication of your diabetes; I'm afraid we're at that place now." As Bob became agitated, the doctor continued, "And we talked before about your diet. It's going to be more important than ever that you follow the meal plan we gave you, and by all means no alcohol. Your kidneys just can't handle that."

"So...I gotta keep coming here like two or three times a week to stay alive? Depend on some machine to live?" Bob challenged. "What kind of life is that?"

"Mr. Wright, I'm sorry, but this is our only option," the doctor firmly concluded.

Later that week on his way back one day from Park Street Church to his apartment, he passed a liquor store. He stopped and thought for a few minutes. Then he went inside to make a purchase. Later that evening, with just the light from the outside streetlight shining in, leaning back against two pillows on his bed, he stared out at exactly nothing in particular. A half-empty bottle of vodka sat on the night stand next to him. He reached over, picked up the bottle and poured another glass and then replaced the bottle on the night stand. While still staring ahead, he lifted the glass slowly to his mouth and drank half of it and then rested the glass on his thigh. Moments later the contents of the glass spilled onto the bed and the glass fell to the floor as it was released from a now lifeless hand. Bob slumped over to one side.

The next day I received a call at work from Jonathan saying that Bob had passed away in his sleep. We were both stunned and couldn't quite comprehend the tragic news. We talked some. Then we agreed that there should be a memorial service for him. It should be at the Park Street Church. We contacted one of the ministers at the church and a memorial service was arranged in the visitors' center on August 20, 2009 at 12:15 p.m. A notice in the corner window of the church behind where Bob used to sit let people know about his passing and that there would be a service for him there on the 20th.

As far as a burial was concerned, since we couldn't locate any family to authorize whether or not Bob's remains could be cremated, he was to be buried in Fair View Cemetery, in what is called the "Lot for the City Poor." The Commonwealth of Massachusetts covers the cost for burial services for the poor in what is their final resting place, adding further insult to injury as they are assured of being forgotten — there is no accommodation to place a stone on their graves. There's just a number placed on the ground with a name on a corresponding list in the office.

As it happened though, one of the members of Hearth's Board of Directors was the director at a funeral home. She helped us make arrangements for a small graveside service. There were some restrictions at the cemetery. "The state agency that oversees these burials," she explained, "has a regulation that prevents the public from going to the actual gravesite itself. But, like you, I don't want to let Bob's passing go unnoticed. I've been able to make arrangements for some of us to go and offer a short graveside remembrance at the cemetery. It will be near the place where he'll be buried. I'll talk with your pastor about the details. We can do this on the 19th. Why don't you plan to call the office next week for final details and to get directions?"

The day before when I called to confirm the arrangements, I found the staff hadn't been told that we were coming. "You can't go there, they don't let the public go. You're not allowed to go," insisted the office attendant on the other end of the phone. My heart sank when I thought there would be no opportunity to say goodbye.

I started, "But I spoke with the funeral director last week and the arrangements have been made and..."

"No you can't go, it's a rule and the public can't go," came the voice more insistently.

On the verge of tears, I asked, "OK, listen, would you please let me speak directly to the director?"

"Yeah, wait a minute," was the surly response, "she's here in her office."

Relieved to hear the director's voice, I began, "I'm a bit puzzled. I must have asked the wrong person in your office about the arrangements for tomorrow. They said I couldn't go, that the public isn't allowed to go."

Reassuringly she said, "Please don't worry, Christina, everything is still all set. I probably hadn't spoken to enough people about it and my staff didn't have all the information about this special case. As I told you we can't go to the actual gravesite where he will be buried, but we can have our service in the cemetery near there; that's what's been arranged."

There were no dignitaries there in the cemetery the next morning, save for the ridge of distinguished evergreens keeping watch on the rise in the distance. A simple, stark, roughly constructed plywood box rested in front of us on the grass. The word "TOP" was written with a black marker on one end with an arrow pointing toward that word. As we stood together on the grounds of Fair View Cemetery in Hyde Park under an azure August sky, the morning mist filtered through an opening in the trees where we could see the Blue Hills dressed in summer's finery. A red-tailed hawk — a fellow mourner — circled in the sky above.

As the temperature rose steadily toward 90 degrees, a handful of us shared memories of a friend who not two weeks ago passed away during the night at the age of 59. The only comfort was that for close to two years at the end of his life he was housed and cared for in Hearth's assisted living center.

The day after the burial the memorial service was held in the Park Street Church visitors' center. Jonathan and I thought there would either be just two of us or the place would be packed. Well, packed it was. Friends, who came to know Bob as they walked to work each weekday morning, as well as church-goers who had befriended, and who had been befriended by Bob Wright packed the Visitor Center at Park Street Church for the service that lasted for over an hour. Bob's obituary took up one-third of a page in the August 16th Sunday Boston Globe Metro section along with two other distinguished Bostonians.

While we couldn't mark Bob's grave in the cemetery where he was buried, I learned that (not coincidentally) someone from my home church had donated a marker in our church's memorial garden for "anyone who needed it." In the fall during a brief outdoor service of remembrance, an engraved stone was placed in the garden near the fountain, and near Sue's marker, as church members gathered around.

For the unenlightened who passed him by each work day on the corner of Park and Tremont Streets in Boston, he was invisible; he was just another guy looking for a handout, living among society's forgotten. But, to those lives he touched with his kindness and hard-earned wisdom, he left an unforgettable legacy, not the least of which included his admonition: "SMILE: It's the Law!"

He *is* remembered.

Final Notes

At the time of Bob's passing, we were unsuccessful in locating any family that we thought should be notified – Bob said he didn't have anyone anymore. But, sadly, it wasn't until a year and a half later on New Year's Eve that Jonathan was contacted by Bob's niece, his brother's daughter, who was living in Florida with her mother. She said her mother had finally shown her the obituary for her Uncle Bob, and she wanted to know if Bob ever spoke about her father. She wanted to know more about him. We told her he did, indeed, talk about his brother and said how he had loved him; about how sad he was that he was gone.

Then, amazingly, in the summer of 2011, I received a note in the mail. It said:

> *Dear Christina, I wondered where he was. Through the strangest of channels that exist in the even stranger universe…I learned about a month ago that he was housed. Today I learned that he had returned. What a magnificent being. I would love to talk with you about him. If you so choose, me in my big, comfortable life…*

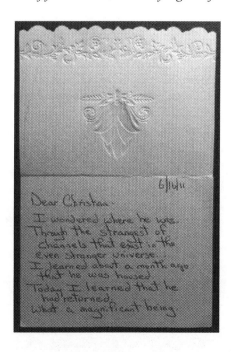

The note was from Bob's former, very significant other whom he had known for several years in the 70's. They spent time together traveling around the country on his motorcycle, together with Beano, his dog riding in the bike's trailer. After several years, they had parted company in Florida, where he remained for a while, and she returned home to New England. At one point Bob had asked me if I might try to locate her via the Internet, but he wasn't sure where she was living and if her name might have changed. But I was unsuccessful. However, after his passing, through "the strangest of channels that exist…" I found that she was living in the Boston area and working as a nurse at *Boston Healthcare for the Homeless*. One day she was working with an elderly client there to see about locating housing. She went on Hearth's website, and was shocked to find a video of Bob (she called him "Robert"), who had been featured on the site. She looked into his story, found the ABC News' "Chronicle" clip about my story and was able to contact me. We did meet on several occasions thereafter, and she was able to fill in some of the pieces of Bob's life.

And then, even more amazingly, in 2016 I received a phone call from one of Bob's step-sisters! She said they (her sisters and a brother) had lost touch with Bob (whom they also called "Robert") about 20 years ago and had learned the news about Bob's passing through yet another cosmic channel. Before she contacted me, she related that she fell asleep before the end of a movie she was watching about baseball player Jimmy Piersall who was treated at Westborough State Hospital (in Massachusetts) for mental illness. She wanted to see if she could find a link to the video somewhere on the Internet so that she could catch the ending. At the same time, she was curious about one of her relatives (not Bob) who had been treated at the same hospital. She entered the person's name together with Westborough Hospital and up popped Bob Wright's story on the Hearth website. She was able to find my contact information from the website as well.

We spoke quite a long time, and I shared my story in coming to know Bob. I learned more about his past, a childhood filled with abuse, neglect and abandonment. She was grateful to have learned that he was finally housed, but sorry not to have known about his circumstances for she surely would have helped him. Mostly she was sorry that he wasn't loved.

Bob's Top 10 Birthday Wish List

Robert "Bob" Wright kept a journal that documented his life living on and off the streets. Over the years he kept a "Top 10 Wish List," a photo of which is included below. His "Number 1 Wish" on every list was always, as he spelled it, "Hope, not dispare."

November 27, 1995

Bob's Newest Top Ten Wish List

10. *Clothes for me – 34-36 waist, 16 ½ - 33 shirt, 7.45 hat, 40 coat.*

9. *People willing to try to help the homeless. Most are willing, they just don't know how.*

8. *Dentist – I am tired of my food coming through a straw.*

7. *Still #7 – Ruby Slippers, Click, Click – "There's no place like home."*

6. *A tiny recorder with tapes – this experience must be documented (a cheap one will not last out here).*

5. *To be treated with RESPECT – most homeless are real people, just blindsided.*

4. *FOOD – this is more important than money. If I get too much I can feed others.*

3. *SMILES and hellos as you walk by. Some days this is all that keeps me going.*

2. *Clean, warm, home.*

1. *Still #1 – Hope, not "dispare"*

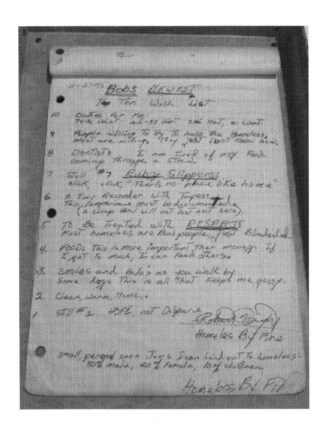

The Crisis of Elder Homelessness

The challenges faced by an individual living without secure, consistent housing can't be overstated. An "elderly" man or woman who is homeless faces a unique set of circumstances, not the least of which includes managing a chronic mental or physical illness.

According to Hearth, Inc. the plight of homeless seniors remains an under-recognized and under-served segment of the homeless population. While in 1990 only 11 percent of adults experiencing homelessness were aged 50 or older, this figure had increased to 32 percent by 2013. The size of the older homeless adult population is projected to almost double over the next decade. The problem is not only tragic, but the health-related implications of an aging homeless population are significant and have cost implications to the health care system. Compared to their younger counterparts and to the general population, homeless adults aged 50 and older have higher rates of medical co-morbidities, functional disability, and geriatric conditions. What's more, these conditions develop 15-20 years earlier for this population than in their housed counterparts.

In addition to this book, a website (www.theparkstreetangels.com) has been created as a vehicle to provide information to youth-serving and community groups, faith communities, health and human service students and providers as well as the general public to:

1. raise awareness of the unique challenges faced by elders who are homeless/ at risk of homelessness

2. demonstrate how Hearth's model program has (1) made a positive impact on the lives of homeless elders in Boston by providing them with outreach and supportive living facilities and (2) inspired and increased development of housing programs like Hearth's in other cities and towns

3. further the understanding of how to prevent homelessness by providing an introduction to the notion of "adverse childhood experiences" (ACEs)

and "toxic stress" and their consequences on early childhood brain development and the increasing risk for mental illness, substance use, homelessness and chronic disease (heart disease, diabetes, cancer, etc.) in adulthood, as well as the concept of "trauma-informed care"

4. provide a few links to agencies and resources for supporting elders who are homeless or at risk of homelessness

Angel with an Attitude

Well, he wasn't there this morning, guess he had something else to do.
I was kind of looking forward to hear his point of view.
He'd tell his joke, he made me laugh, he went the extra mile.
And the sign that sat there next to him said, "It's the law: SMILE"

The first time that I saw him, I quickly walked on by.
The next day I encountered him, he looked me in the eye.
I turned away, afraid to see; went on along my way.
Then I looked back as I walked on. His eyes had so much to say.

They were tired and full of aging, but the message still came through
as if he was some angel, disguised to look like me or you.
Maybe it's some paradox, and, in reality, like so many other angels,
they're invisible unless you want to see.

Next day when I saw him, I finally came prepared.
Some quarters that I set aside, left over from my fare,
were waiting in my pocket, hoping there he'd be.
It took a lot of gumption; this was something new for me.

He sat outside the church at Park Street right near the Park Street "T."
He'd "set up shop" like he does most days, but, of concern to see,
another sign placed next to him said, "Homeless by Fire."
I handed him the quarters, he said, "Thank you, Ma'am," and smiled.

So I smiled and muttered something and then walked on my way,
and, as I went about my work, I thought of him all day.
What's it like to be out there? And soberly I'd muse:
Could I really walk in his shoes?

He could be a character from Steinbeck living in some hard-luck tale,
but he also looked like "St. Nick" with his white beard and long hair.
But how dare I romanticize his grim reality?
I pay a price when I discount his full humanity.

The next day that I saw him, with two dollars more to spare,
I said, "I'm sorry for your trouble," and, as I lingered there,
it occurred to me to ask him 'bout his work in former times.
Said he was a coppersmith way back in his prime.

He worked on roofs and steeples [I'm sure a master of his trade].
He said that, of his people, he was the only one remained.
And illness now had taken hold, he had the "sugar blues."
Then he relented, "Now, this is all that I can do."

I asked him where he stayed at night. [I didn't mean to pry.]
He didn't mind my asking, and said he stayed in the subway.
"Do they give you any trouble?" He said, "Oh, no, not me!
It's all about my attitude; they let me be."

Then I asked him where'd he get his care? [Thought that I could helpful be.]
Said he'd found some friendly doctors over at Mass "G."
They gave him drugs and insulin – shot up four times a day.
Living on his attitude, he didn't have to pay.

He told me that he could stay healthy if he can only get some food.
Living in the streets like this, it was hard to test his blood.
But "table scraps" from garbage cans sustained him every day.
I wondered if he had the faith to pray.

For what it was worth I told him, said I could somehow empathize –
I'd been out of work for half a year, but, lest I trivialize
his present situation; it might have been mine.
When there was doubt my hard times would ever end,
(with the help of some gracious friends)
there, but for the grace of God, was I.
There, but for the grace of God, was I.

You might ask, "What's in it for you?" Or you might ask me how I know
that he isn't trying to con me to buy smokes and alcohol.
The answer's very simple, but, a paradox you see:
it's kind of like forgiveness – I'm doing this for me.

Maybe I'll see him tomorrow. I wonder what he'll have to say.
Will he smile and tell the same old joke, or will he find another way
to live and keep on seeking his winter heart's desire?
But, perhaps, that's as an angel there beneath the Park Street spire.

Angel with an Attitude by Christina Nordstrom is featured on "North Stream"
at www.christinanordstrom.bandcamp.com.